THE USEFUL MUSICIAN

101 Ways To Improve Yourself
And Get Asked Back

by Ed Schief

FOREWORD

The world has enough rock stars. The world also has enough books about how to be a rock star. We also have a surplus of players who *think* they're rock stars.

You know what we *do* need? We need more players on our own local scenes who can fit in, who can contribute in a variety of situations and who make every group of musicians they join *sound better.* The world needs useful musicians.

The world needs musicians who show up and get the job done, who understand how the music goes together, who know where they fit in and what to do to make a song sound good.

We local players are part of that 'great unwashed mass' who will never be famous, never make a living as a musician, never sign an autograph and never shout 'Thank you Cleveland!' into a 1.3 gigawatt PA system. We perform in bars, churches, restaurants and coffee houses, we do it because it's fun, and we know by now there's never going to be any real money.

I've played in clubs and recording studios, produced a handful of local CD's, ran an instrumental music program at a big church, ran a cover band for several years and in general have found my way into a pretty big variety of playing situations. I've even brushed up briefly against the famous and near-famous. But here I am after all this time, working at an auto parts store and playing weekends off and on for not really a whole lot of money.

So I started a couple of years ago writing down everything I could think of that might help someone with less experience. There's no college education here. Everything I'm presenting is something I learned because I needed to know it to keep moving forward. These are things I've learned by keeping my eyes and ears open, by asking questions, by trying and failing and trying again.

Persistence, it turns out, is a pretty good substitute for talent.

Like your dad, I'm hoping you won't repeat the mistakes I've made. I hope you'll keep improving, and find yourself becoming A Useful Musician.

INTRODUCTION

I purposely did NOT write this book as a linear, 'Big Idea' presentation. Instead, I mean this book to be something you can dip into. Most of the musicians I respect don't come at it in a linear fashion anyway. Yeah, you can go to a music school and get it formally (something I might do when I retire, just for the kick of it), but who has time for that? Everybody I know, everybody I play with (local, day-job musicians), they learn a little, apply it, learn a little more, etc. And frankly, I'm always a little suspicious of musicians who are, well...'over-linear'. Playing music is not an entirely logical pursuit.

I've also tried to keep this book useful for *any* musician, but here and there I found myself talking directly to keyboardists and guitar players, or using those instruments to make a point. I couldn't think of a way around that—keys and guitar are the two instruments I'm proficient on. But it's all connected, it's all music, it's all something you'll be glad you're familiar with. Getting a broad picture, knowing how everything goes together is a very valuable thing, in my opinion. The best musicians I know are pretty familiar with the other instruments in the band, even the ones they don't play.

Also, I repeat myself occasionally. If you find yourself saying, 'Didn't he address this a couple pages back?', just roll with it. If something is important enough, I think coming at it more than once doesn't hurt.

Okay, if I *do* have one overarching theme here, it would be this:

> *Pay attention and you can improve, even if you're not super-talented. The more you know about how good music is put together, the more useful you'll be.*

Of course, none of this will do you any good if you don't apply it. So get out and play!

TABLE OF CONTENTS

Chapter 1-Practice

#1—SING ALONG WITH WHAT YOU PLAY

#2—LEARN TO HEAR THE 1'S

#3—KEEP YOUR INSTRUMENT IN YOUR HANDS

#4—THINK OF MINOR 7 CHORDS AS A MAJOR OVER A ROOT

#5—LEARN THE BLUES SCALE

#6—PRACTICE THE MAJOR SCALE

#7—PRACTICE ARPEGGIOS

#8—INVEST IN PRACTICE TRACKS

#9—PRACTICE WITH A METRONOME

#10—PRACTICE THE HARD PARTS

Chapter 2-Rehearsal

#11—LISTEN TO THE SONG IN THE CAR

#12—MAKE YOUR MUSIC EASIER TO READ

#13—DON'T OVERREHEARSE

#14—SIMPLIFY. ALWAYS SIMPLIFY

#15—MOVE TO AN EASIER KEY

#16—DON'T ASSUME THE WRITTEN MUSIC IS RIGHT

#17—MAKE A CAPO CHART

#18—ASK TO TALK THE SONG THROUGH BEFORE YOU PLAY IT

#19—EXPLOIT UNEXPECTED THINGS

#20—TIE SOMETHING UNRELATED INTO MEMORIZATION

#21—LOOK OVER THE WRITTEN MUSIC AHEAD OF TIME

#22—TAPE YOUR MUSIC TOGETHER

#23—REWRITE THE MUSIC YOU'RE GIVEN

#24—PLAN TO PERFORM AT ABOUT 2/3 OF YOUR CAPACITY

Chapter 3-Onstage

#25—STOP BLAMING YOUR EQUIPMENT

#26—STICK AND MOVE

#27—SET A NEW TEMPO BY SINGING IN YOUR HEAD

#28—BUILDING BLOCKS FIRST, SPECIFICS SECOND

#29—THE AUDIENCE LISTENS WITH THEIR EYES

#30—EMBRACE BEING ONSTAGE

#31—SHOW UP ON TIME

#32—SIMPLIFY YOUR MONITOR MIX

#33—EXPECT SURPRISES

#34—SERVE THE SONG FIRST, THE AUDIENCE SECOND,
        YOURSELF LAST

#35—EXAGGERATE DYNAMICS

#36—PLAY THE EMOTION OF THE SONG

#37—LEAVE ROOM FOR OTHER PLAYERS

#38—TELEGRAPH THE WHOLE SONG WITH YOUR INSTRUMENT

#39—DON'T WARM UP IN EVERYONE'S FACE

#40—BRING OPTIONS TO THE SONG

#41—FIGURE OUT THE OTHER PLAYERS

#42—ONLY PLAY NOTES THAT MAKE MONEY

#43—LEARN TO READ BODY LANGUAGE

#44—STOP BEING CLEVER

#45—MAKE FRIENDS WITH THE AUDIENCE

#46—PLAY CONFIDENTLY

#47—BE SENSITIVE TO OTHER PLAYERS' SHORTCOMINGS

#48—DON'T LOSE CONCENTRATION DURING REPEATED

PERFORMANCES

#49—THINK OF THE ACOUSTIC GUITAR AS A PERCUSSION
    INSTRUMENT THAT PLAYS NOTES

#50—SET UP SO YOU CAN SEE EVERYBODY

#51—CAPITALIZE ON UNEXPECTED THINGS

#52—DON'T SLAVISHLY COPY THE ORIGINAL RECORDING

#53—MOVE UP AND DOWN TO STAY OUT OF
    THE SINGER'S RANGE

#54—PLAY THE ROOM

#55—PLAY IT IN YOUR OWN VOICE

#56—PLAY IN THE MOMENT

#57—LEAVE YOUR EGO IN THE PARKING LOT

#58—SELL THE SONG

#59—FIND OUT WHAT THE AUDIENCE WANTS

#60—SET YOUR INSTRUMENT LOUD AND THEN CONTROL IT

#61—USE THE COUNT-IN TO SET THE FEEL
    IN EVERYONE'S BONES

#62—THINK LIKE AN ARRANGER

Chapter 4-Leading A Band

#63—SIMPLIFY THE CHORDS

#64—TELL THE STORY

#65—PLAY TO YOUR MUSICIAN'S STRENGTHS

#66—GET RID OF TRICKY RHYTHMIC PASSAGES

#67—DIVIDE RHYTHMS AND RANGES

#68—BUILD THE SONG FROM THE BOTTOM UP

#69—MAKE THE INTRO A REPEATING LOOP

#70—USE THE INTRO TO SET UP THE FEEL

#71—LAY YOUR CHARTS OUT LOGICALLY, 4 BARS PER LINE

#72—DIRECT INSTEAD OF MEMORIZING

#73—MAKE ROOM FOR A MUSICIANS' CREATIVITY

Chapter 5-General Musicianship

#74—LISTEN AND LEARN ABOUT OTHER INSTRUMENTS
#75—LEARN A NEW SONG EVERY WEEK
#76—MAKE SURE YOUR EQUIPMENT WORKS
#77—LISTEN TO OLDER MUSIC
#78—EDUCATE YOURSELF ABOUT SOUND
#79—DON'T EVER BE TOO GOOD FOR A SONG
#80—LENGTHEN YOUR PHRASES
#81—PLAY INTO THE GROOVE
#82—LEARN TO LOVE THE GROOVE
#83—EMPHASIZE ALONG WITH THE SNARE
#84—PLAY ON THE BACK OF THE BEAT
#85—THINK OF DYNAMICS AS ADDING AND SUBTRACTING ENERGY
#86—PLAY SHORTER OR LONGER NOTES TO ADD OR SUBTRACT ENERGY
#87—SHORTEN NOTES TO ADD ENERGY
#88—TELL THE TRUTH
#89—LEARN TO RECOVER
#90—FLIP THE SWITCH
#91—DO THE JOB ONLY YOU CAN DO
#92—CHANGE YOUR DEFINITION OF SUCCESS
#93—THINK LIKE YOUR LISTENER
#94—LISTEN FOR THE MAGIC
#95—TAKE RESPONSIBILITY FOR WHAT YOU PLAY
#96—FLOAT ABOVE THE MUSIC
#97—LEARN TO COUNT
#98—LEARN TO HEAR IN MULTIPLES OF TWO
#99—DEVELOP A THICK SKIN
#100—GET BETTER AT PLAYING WHEN YOU CAN'T HEAR YOURSELF
#101—STOP THINKING OF EVERYTHING AS MYSTERIOUS

CHAPTER 1 - PRACTICE

I struggle with this like everyone else. I work at my playing, it gets better. I stop working at it, my abilities drift down. Even my ear gets rusty. When this happens, I have to rely on my talent to get me through. Sometimes it's enough, sometimes...not.

I sat down at a friends' new grand piano the other day, thought I'd do an impromptu song or two, and I couldn't get 'Somewhere Over The Rainbow' into my fingers. I looked at my wife and said, "I CAN'T FIND IT!". The reason was simple—I haven't sat at keyboard and played what's in my head for quite a while.

You gotta work at it, and you gotta work at it when nobody's looking. The best motivation I've found is having an actual gig. You're playing this Friday night or Sunday morning, you want to do it well. So I'll repeat my advice from the introduction—get out and play! Do that, and you'll have a reason to discipline yourself.

#1—SING ALONG WITH WHAT YOU PLAY

WHY IT MAKES YOU MORE USEFUL:

It teaches you to hear a note before you play it. This enables you to more easily play what's in your head. Also, it greatly improves your phrasing, which makes your playing more interesting.

WHAT TO DO:

Start by just playing a simple scale—the major scale, the pentatonic scale, the blues scale, whatever. Go slowly and sing along. Try moving back and forth as you go, moving up, then down a little, then back up some more.

Invest in background tracks made for improv practice. Pick a slow track and play long notes at first. Next try skipping notes, jumping to a note farther up or down the scales. Be aware of your singing and breathing and how it affects your playing. If you can't do it the first time, keep trying. Like anything else, you'll get better at this the more you do it.

When you've gained a little confidence, try this onstage, in front of real people. They'll never hear you, and if they see your lips moving, they'll think you're being an *artiste.*

When you can hear something in your head and then play it without missing a note, you've crossed over from playing patterns and memorized motifs to real, honest improvising. Real improvising comes from your head, not your hands.

Also, this improves the phrasing, or musicality of your improvising. When you sing, you have to pause to breathe. If you're singing along with what you're playing, you'll naturally pause your playing while you pause to breathe. This goes a long way toward curing a run-on style of improvising. Even 4 bars of constant 8th or 16th notes is tedious and boring. Singing along forces you to think in phrases, and will result in much, much better sounding solos and other little things you might improvise.

Lastly, it internalizes everything. You need the music to start from inside *you*, not your instrument. Ideally, you should never, ever be surprised by something that comes out of your instrument. It should start inside you and work it's way out into your instrument.

This is partly about training your ear and partly about learning to connect the notes your hear with the physical act of playing your instrument. You hear a note in your head, and then you feel where it is on your instrument. You connect the two.

THOUGHTS:

There was a time I couldn't do this. I clearly remember sitting at my parents' piano, trying to play the melody to a Christmas carol without any music. I could hear the melody in my head, but I couldn't get it into my hands. I'd find the first note, then sing the next note, then try to find it on the keyboard. I'd miss every time, or if I hit one right, I was just lucky. It really, really frustrated me.

And then one day in my high school band class, the band director said, "Can you hear the notes in your head before you play them?"

He had my undivided attention.

"We'll start with the interval of a fourth. For instance, a C up to an F. Does that sound like anything you've heard? It should— it's the opening to 'Here Comes The Bride'. If you see an interval of a fourth on the music, then start on the first note, hum 'Here Comes The Bride', and you'll know how the second note should sound."

I tried it, and it worked. I went home and sat at the piano playing random note after random note, then singing 'Here Comes The Bride' starting on that note.

That day he also gave us other songs for other intervals ('My Bonnie' for a major 6), and let me tell you—I felt like he'd let me in on a priceless secret. I'd listen to songs on the radio or my record player and try to identify the intervals. After a while I got pretty good at it, and found that my ability to pick out a melody on the piano was getting much faster.

I'm pretty good at it after all these years, but only on piano and in my head. The guitar is an entirely different animal, and I have a long way to go on THAT instrument. So I work at it.

Ed Schief

Sometimes when I'm driving in my car or the work truck, I'll think of a melody and see if I can play it on the guitar neck—in my head. I get it wrong a lot, but every once in a while I'll get a revelation and think, "Okay, that little nugget was worth missing my turn."

Be curious.

#2—LEARN TO
HEAR THE 1'S

WHY IT MAKES YOU
MORE USEFUL:

You'll seldom lose your place in the music.

WHAT TO DO:

The downbeat is the first beat in any measure. If you can hear this, you can always find your place in a rhythmic sense. This just takes practice. Pick a simple song, and as you're listening, say the word 'one' on every first beat. Then get it into your body by tapping your foot on every downbeat. Do this enough and you'll make it second nature, hearing FAR more easily where sections of the song start, where the chords fall, etc.

The '1 chord' is the chord that names the key you're in. In the key of E, E is the one chord. This is a little harder to do than hearing the downbeat, but you can do it.

Start with the chords to a familiar song, one that you know is in a particular key. Keep the chords in front of you, and every time the 1 chord comes around, say the word 'one' out loud. There's a particular sound, or weight to the 1 chord. It's the home base chord. It's the chord that feels 'settled'. You might have a different way of defining that 'home base' sound and feeling, but pretty soon you'll be hearing and feeling it much more easily.

THOUGHTS:

This is about training your ear. If you can hear and feel both of these, you'll be pretty unshakeable in terms of keeping your place and learning songs more quickly.

#3—KEEP YOUR INSTRUMENT IN YOUR HANDS

WHY IT MAKES YOU MORE USEFUL:

Daily practice makes your playing more fluid. When things are a little easier to execute, it makes the sound coming out of your instrument more pleasing. Doing it every day, or nearly, breaks up the logjam of clumsy hands and fingers.

WHAT TO DO:

Set aside a time every day, or several times a week to play your instrument and work on your playing. Set up a place where you always practice, and keep everything set up so you can just walk in and start. This eliminates the excuse 'I don't feel like setting everything up'. I'm the KING of this, so I built a bench in my basement, and my stuff is always set up. I flip a switch, put on my guitar, and I'm up and running. Do this, and you can even sneak in five or ten minutes while you're waiting for your ride, or your spouse to get out of the shower, or whatever.

THOUGHTS:

Daniel Coyle, in his excellent book 'The Little Book Of Talent', talks about 'soft skills' and 'hard skills'. A soft skill is something you work to understand. A hard skill is something you work to execute. You can watch a video about golf and learn the fundamentals of the swing (the soft skill), but the hard skill is actually swinging the club, which takes...wait for it...practice. Practice can be dry, I know. Elsewhere in this book I'll give you some ideas for practicing that might make it a little more fun, but let me tell you what's NOT dry: pulling off something onstage that makes you and everybody else grin.

I saw saxophonist Justo Almario speak live, and he told us he walks around the house with just the mouthpiece of his sax, blowing long, long notes. He works to make them consistent in volume and pitch. Yeah, it makes his family a little crazy. But if you've heard him play, you can hear those beautiful tones coming out of his instrument and you KNOW his embouchure is strong like a weight lifter. Like he could bench press 350 with his lips. He can hold notes all day, and that makes his tone so smooth, so consistent.

Most of us don't have all kinds of spare time waiting to be filled. I know how it is. So be consistent, be purposeful in your practicing and I promise you'll be happy with the results.

As I write this, I'm experiencing this very thing. I haven't picked up my guitar, sadly, in several months. I'm performing Dick Dale's 'Misirlou' in a couple of weeks, which requires that really fast, staccato tremolo. I ran through it several nights ago and I COULDN'T DO THE FAST PICKING. Like, at all. I panicked a little. I've been hit-

ting it for five minutes every morning and night for a few days, and I think I'll be okay. It'd be good if I followed my own advice.

#4—THINK OF MI7 CHORDS AS A MAJOR OVER A ROOT

WHY IT MAKES YOU MORE USEFUL:

It throws the door open to new ways of playing the same old chords.

WHAT TO DO:

(I couldn't resist throwing this in, despite it being a little more in-depth. Save it for later if it seems like too much.)

This is an easy concept, but you'll have to work through it.
Basically this: Think of minor 7 chords as a major chord over a different root. Start from the root of the chord and count up three half steps. When you get there, use that note as the root of a major chord. So you'd think of a Cmi7 as an Eb major chord

over a C bass. Another way to write it would be Eb/C.

There are basically 12 of these, one for each step of the scale, *(17, if you count the chords that can be written either as a sharp or flat chord). The ones listed here are the most common ones. Here's all the info you really need:*

Cmi7 = Eb/C

C#mi7 - E/C

Dmi7 = F/D

Ebmi7 = Gb/Eb

Emi7 = G/E

Fmi7 = Ab/F

F#mi7 - A/F#

Gbmi7 = A/Gb (Yeah, I know it's supposed to be B double flat. NOBODY does this)

Gmi7 = Bb/G

G#mi7 - B/G#

Abmi7 = B/Ab (Again..)

Ami7 = C/A

A#mi7 = C#/A#

Bbmi7 - Db/Bb

Bmi7 = D/B

Here's why this is SO USEFUL:

When you're playing with a bass player, you don't need to play the bass note of a chord—it's already covered. So just play the top three notes and think of them as a major chord. For example: An Ami7 chord is really a C chord with an A in the bass. So play a C chord and leave the bass note out of it. Stop thinking you HAVE to play all four notes. You don't. When you play the top three notes and the bass player plays the bottom note, the audience hears the whole chord. Simple as that. This makes your playing cleaner and gives you all KINDS of options for where to play the chord. Also, it makes your chords sound a little more open, not so thick. Makes more room in the sound.

Pick an easy song, one you know, and try this out. Rewrite the mi7 chords as slash chords, then play along with the recording just adding in those major chords. As soon as you get the hang of it, start including it whenever you can in your performing. Rewrite the chords in the music you're given, until you can remember them better. Don't try to memorize all in one bite. Pick a few of these, start using them. When you have those, add others.

BONUS:

You can do the same thing with major 7 (ma7) chords. Same exact thing, except it's minor chords over a bass note. Here's the plan:

> Cma7 = Emi/C
> Dbma7 - Fmi/Db
> Dma7 = F#mi/D
> Ebma7 = Gmi/Eb
> Ema7 = G#mi/E
> Fma7 = Ami/F
> Gbma7 - Bbmi/Gb
> Gma7 = Bmi/G
> Abma7 = Cmi/Ab
> Ama7 = C#mi/A
> Bbma7 = Dmi/Bb
> Bma7 = D#mi/B

THOUGHTS:

When I saw this, when I figured it out, it changed EVERY-THING for me. My playing on keys immediately improved, later my guitar playing. Here are two easy examples:

On guitar: Instead of playing your normal position for Ami7, play a four string C chord up at the 8th fret. (Like a beginner F, but up at the 8th fret). The bass will fill in the A on the bottom.

On piano: Play the Ami7 as an A bass note in your left hand, down low, and a C chord higher up.

#5—LEARN THE BLUES SCALE

WHY IT MAKES YOU MORE USEFUL:

Because it's everywhere. It permeates nearly every style of music other than classical--it's buried in plain sight in a million songs. Get familiar with it and you'll get your head inside a song much faster, improvise better and remember passages from songs much more easily.

WHAT TO DO:

Here's the blues scale, drawn from the notes in the major scale:

1, b3, 4, 5b, 5, b7, 1

And that's it. In the key of C it would be:

C, Eb, F, Gb, G, Bb, C

There are warehouses full of books about this—buy one and get started.

Practice playing the blues scale—a lot—and then play along with practice tracks. You can find these tracks on youtube, but there are others available to download. You won't need to look hard or long to find what you need.

When you need to play something in a song—an intro, ending, turnaround, solo, something interesting, etc., this is almost always the perfect place to start.

Here's the kicker: You can use this same exact scale to get a sweeter, more major feel by moving it down three half steps. Works like magic. So if you're playing a song in G, but the blues scale feels too aggressive for the song, play the E blues scale instead, over the same chords, still in G.

Using the blues scale in these two ways will open up a world of improvising possibilities for you.

THOUGHTS:

You can't believe how useful this is. Here's an example. I was filling in for a friend, running the band at his church on a Sunday. We were doing a performance number, and I was standing next to a guitar player I knew from working in the guitar shop. He had good hands on the guitar, and a decent grasp of music theory, but he was in the weeds on this song.

When the song leader stopped for a minute to work on vocals, I leaned over and said, "We need a little something in the four bars between the first and second verses. Just a little something. Then, we need it after the first chorus, as we circle back into the 3rd verse. Then after the 2nd chorus there's that 8 bar stretch where we play instrumentally—that's all you. Then, when the last chorus comes in after that, keep soloing behind the singer. Play little things that sort of call and answer with whatever she's singing. If she holds a long note, play a little something."

He said, "Okay, but...I don't know what to play."

I said, "The song is in Bb, so plant your first finger at the 6th fret and just STAY there, playing notes out of the blues scale whenever something's needed."

And he did. In fact, I remember thinking he did a really good job of it. He played all kinds of little things, and they dressed the song up wonderfully.

THAT'S what you can do with the blues scale.

#6—PRACTICE THE MAJOR SCALE

WHY IT MAKES YOU MORE USEFUL:

Everything, and I mean everything that has to do with notes and pitches—every scale, every mode, every key signature, every chord—comes from this scale. It's the bedrock of all Western music. All of it. It's like memorizing the alphabet. Knowing it in your head and ears and hands will make everything else come easier. Lots easier.

WHAT TO DO:

Practice it over and over on your instrument, in every key. Start your practice time with it. On most instruments (piano, wind instruments) there's only one way to play each major scale. On the guitar it's a different story. But whatever the case, start doing it. There are books about this, lots of resources. I used to play it on the guitar starting on the third fret, sixth string (G), up two octaves to the first string, and then up a fret and back down in Ab. And so on. Take literally five minutes every time you practice to do this.

THOUGHTS:

A long time ago somebody told me they say this in Army infantry training: "Take good care of your shovel and your shovel will take good care of you." That sentiment applies here. Learn the major scale in every key (come on, it's not that hard, and besides, quit making excuses) and you'll have made the best musical friend you could make. Everything you play will sound a little more familiar, and that's because everything you play comes from the major scale. All of it.

Did you know that chords are organized into keys? All the chords in every key come from the major scale in that key. Have you heard of modes? They're all drawn from the major scale. The Dorian mode is a major scale that starts on the second note of the major scale instead of the first. Some of that stuff is complicated, but I tell you just to make a point—it all starts with the major scale. Get it into your bones. It doesn't make things harder, it makes them easier.

#7—PRACTICE ARPEGGIOS

WHY IT MAKES YOU MORE USEFUL:

Arpeggios are just the notes of a chord played out one by one. Practice them, and when you're asked to improvise something, you can at least look at the chord symbols on the page and play the notes of each chord as it goes by. It makes a wonderful jumping off point for improvising, and it will get you through a tight spot when things are happening really fast and you're having trouble keeping up. Use them also as an alternative to strumming or playing full chords. Run the arpeggios of a chord instead and it gives the song a different flavor. Also, you'll hear chords and chord changes more easily.

WHAT TO DO:

Practice them as they appear grouped together in keys. Start easy. If you're new to this, you have a little learning curve ahead of you, but the good news is that this stuff is all available in books. All written out, making it pretty easy. In the key of C, for instance, you'd practice playing the notes in a C chord, an F chord and a G chord. That's a good start. Play them up and down the register of your instrument, getting them into your fingers, ears and mind. Then move on to other keys. Do it by rote at first, and it will eventually start seeping into your musical vocabulary.

Once you're become a little conversant with these, and memorized a few, try playing them along with a practice track. Find a simple background track with just three chords, and as each chord comes, play an arpeggio for that chord. Play half notes until you get better at it, then move to quarters, eighths, etc. After that, start playing the notes with varying rhythms, something that dips into the feel of the song.

Sing along while you do this and you'll start owning those notes.

THOUGHTS:

It's boring, practicing things like scales and arpeggios. I know that. Thinking of it as eating your musical vegetables. You will NOT be sorry you did this. Do it in small doses.

#8—INVEST IN PRACTICE TRACKS

WHY IT MAKES YOU MORE USEFUL:

It exposes your weaknesses. Think you can pull off that scale or arpeggio or really cool lick easily? Think you got it, no sweat? Put on a practice track and see if you can do it three times in a row, every time the changes comes around, no mistakes. You'll know immediately whether you have it or not, because the track won't wait for you to get ready. You can do it or you can't.

Also, with a practice track you get the feel of playing with a band. It allows you to practice in a song-like setting, but without the distractions. Practice tracks tend to be very straightforward, without weird little rhythmic passages, odd numbers of measures, unexpected chords, etc., so you can focus on whatever it is you're trying to improve.

WHAT TO DO:

These things are available all over the internet. You can

download them into iTunes, buy them as CD's, etc. Your local music store might have them as well. Find a genre that fits what you're doing, and pull the trigger. A set of blues practice tracks is a good place to start, or country style, because they tend to keep the chords simpler. But you can find them in any genre, as difficult or as easy as you want.

Practice scales, arpeggios, etc., along with a track, and then improvise along. A twelve bar blues track will look something like this:

```
C --- | ---- | ---- | ---- |
F --- | ---- |C --- | ---- |
G --- |F --- |C --- | ---- |
```

First time through, play the C Blues Scale along with the track, all the way through. As you move through the song, speed up your scale, switching from half notes to quarters, to eighths, etc., as the track progresses.

Then play the track again and practice arpeggios along with it. During the C chord, play a C arpeggio, then switch to an F arpeggio when the F chord comes along, and so forth. You get the idea.

Then do it again and start improvising. This is a GREAT little 10-15 minute warm up, or if you're pressed for time.

And as always—sing along with your improvising.

THOUGHTS:

It's oh, oh so easy to practice something and think you have it, only to get up onstage and realize you don't. I had a chance to play onstage with Phil Keaggy, the legendary Christian guitar-ist. Just one night. He's a monster, and it was a blast. But at one point during the afternoon rehearsal, he waved his arms in the middle of a song and stopped the band. Then he sat playing one particular passage over and over. Finally one of us said, "Are we playing it wrong?". He said, "Oh, no, sorry. Give me a second— I forgot how to play this song. That's what I get for making records in my basement."

Joe, the musical mentor I mention other places in this book, said, "Practicing is like studying, performing is like taking the test."

Playing along with a backing track is the next best thing to performing. Maybe its biggest benefit is that it exposes your weaknesses without wasting anyone else's time.

#9—PRACTICE WITH A METRONOME

WHY IT MAKES YOU MORE USEFUL:

Like practicing with background tracks, it exposes your weaknesses in any given exercise, passage or song (in other words, it keeps you honest), and it improves your sense of tempo. Because you're not tied to a practice track, you can move the tempo up and down and do a little more stopping and starting.

WHAT TO DO:

Set a metronome beat every time you run through a scale, an arpeggio or a tricky passage from a song you're trying to learn. Let's say you're working on the major scale in a particular key. Once you feel you've mastered it, set a slow metronome tempo and play the scale along with it. No mistakes? Speed it up by 4 beats per minute and run the scale again. Keep this up until you find yourself making mistakes, then dial it back 4 bpm and work it again. Figure out why and how you're tripping up. You might first uncover a particular fingering that gives you fits. Fix that, work the correction at a slower tempo until you have it, then bump the tempo up again. Next you might discover that you have a bad habit in one or the other hand. Slow down and fix it.

You might find a problem that takes days or weeks to fix. Count your blessings—you might have gone years without knowing it, or lived your whole life thinking 'I guess I'm just not good enough to play that song'.

Do this every time your practice, and you'll find yourself getting faster and better. You'll also have a way of measuring your progress. You'll KNOW where your weaknesses are because the increasing tempo will expose them.

THOUGHTS:

A while back I was making drumbeats on my synth and recording them to use with my students. I wanted a particular 4/4 pattern in every tempo from 60 to about 140, stepping up 4bpm every time. So I had to sit through three minutes of the same drumbeat at every tempo while I recorded them.

After the first two or three I was supremely bored, and I thought, "Well, why not at least practice along with them?". So I picked a riff on the guitar that always gave me trouble. For three minutes at every tempo, I worked that riff over and over. The results, to me, were borderline stunning. By the time I got to 140 bpm I was absolutely ripping through that riff. I could hardly believe how fast I was playing it.

The metronome really is a sort of secret weapon. Seriously. Yeah, it's a little nerdy, but so is sitting in the audience watching somebody else play and thinking 'Gee, I wish I played like that.'

#10—PRACTICE THE HARD PARTS

WHY IT MAKES YOU MORE USEFUL:

I gotta explain this?

WHAT TO DO:

Break it down into manageable chunks, set your metronome for a slow tempo, and start working up to doing it right. Stop hiding from something you can't play. If you can't play it, admit it and then figure out what's wrong. Pick it apart, find what's holding you back and then fix it.

THOUGHTS:

Sometimes it's a problem in your head. If you can't hear a tricky rhythm, try writing out the rhythm in simple form on a piece of notebook paper.

Here's an example:

My band played the song 'I Want To Take You Higher' by Sly & The Family Stone. There was a horn part we wanted to mimic with the guitars and keys. I tried a few times to get it right, but it was just stumping me. So I listened very carefully, counted, and wrote it down. It's only two bars, so I wrote down the counting for two bars of 8th notes:

| 1 + 2 + 3 + 4 + | 1 + 2 + 3 + 4 + |

Then I listened carefully (several times), counting on my fingers, and marked where the hits were (underlined here):

| <u>1</u> + 2 + 3 <u>+</u> 4 + | 1 + 2 <u>+ 3</u> + 4 +|

Then I said out loud, about six times,

> "ONE and two and three AND four and
> one and two AND THREE and four and"

I practiced the hits with my right hand on my leg while I was counting out loud, faster and faster until I was up to the right tempo. I did it until it started to feel familiar.

Do you see? Break the problem down and kick its butt.

And sometimes the problem is in your hands. I wanted to play the opening to 'Hot Rod Lincoln', but man that's some fast flat picking. So I figured out the lick (there's a youtube of it by the guy who actually played it), listening and watching very carefully, then I matched the tempo on a metronome. It was fast, something like 130 bpm. Then I found the tempo I could

play it, which was about 90 bpm. I worked out the easiest fingering for it. I played it over and over and over until I was comfortable at 90 bpm. Then I moved it up to 94 and started again.
It took me three weeks, but I started to actually play it close to
the original tempo.

I'm not a genius or anywhere close, but I am persistent.

Don't be easy on yourself, and don't make excuses. I know
a lot of musicians, and many of them could be better, but they
just don't really try, you know? Their identity is so wrapped up
in it that they can't admit there's something they can't get right
without really working. Don't be proud—be a problem solver.
And then, when someone says, "Wow, it must be nice to be so
talented. You're so lucky.", you can say, "Thank you. Yes it is.
I'm just lucky."

And finally, this advice from my mother, calling to me from
the kitchen as I practiced the organ after school: "Stop practicing the parts you already know and start practicing the parts
you DON'T know."

CHAPTER 2
REHEARSAL

Good GRIEF I've been through a lot of rehearsals. There is, in my opinion, a little bit of an art to running a good rehearsal. And, oh man—I've been in way, way too many rehearsals that were just a waste of time. You can get a LOT done in a short time, if you stay focused. That begs the question—focus on what? Read on.

#11—LISTEN TO THE SONG IN THE CAR

WHY IT MAKES YOU MORE USEFUL:

The more you hear the song, the better it will stick in your mind. The better it sticks in your mind, the more comfortable you'll be with it, and then you can start adding the cool stuff.

WHAT TO DO:

When you need to be ready for a particular song, listen to it while you drive. Listen to the song on your way to work, at least once during the day, and again on your way home.

THOUGHTS:

Sometimes you just don't like the song. I sympathize, but remember—your goal is to be useful, to do a good job. When this happens, listen more intently. Imagine yourself inside that band in the recording, reacting and playing along with them. Do your best to immerse yourself in the song.

I talked with a drummer a while back who played a lot in various churches. He'd start cramming for the service a day or two before, and he'd have his wife drive him to the church so he could listen and make notes on the music while they drove. He'd absolutely cram the songs into his short-term memory, and then forget them on his way home.

#12—MAKE YOUR
MUSIC EASIER TO READ

WHY IT MAKES YOU
MORE USEFUL:

A clear music sheet eliminates wondering where you are in the song, and it reminds you of important things.

WHAT TO DO:

Circle all the signs, to start with. The D.S. signs, Coda signs, etc. Get a pencil and circle them. Darken anything you think you might miss. Draw big lines—anything that will catch your eye and remind you where you're going. Also, make some kind of note that alerts you to tricky parts or things you really, really need to remember. It's not amateurish to do this. It's just the opposite. A professional does whatever is necessary to play the part right. Ask permission to photocopy the music, then toss it when you're done.

THOUGHTS:

In high school I played trombone in the pit band for our school's presentation of The Sound Of Music. In one spot on my music someone had drawn a little pair of eyeglasses with eyeballs looking down. I raised my hand and asked the Mr. Bartman what those were for. He said, "We rented this music. This is the actual music you'd play if you were on Broadway. Someone used that same music in their own production, and they were setting an alert to themselves about something in that measure. It's part of the rental agreement—you're allowed to draw on the music in pencil if you erase it before you send it back. They obviously forgot to erase it."

I was floored. I thought the big time musicians just *remembered* everything.

On my own music I often make the repeat signs huge with a pencil. They stick out way above and below the staff. If it says 'repeat to bar 16' in tiny little letters, I write, in big letters, 'BACK TO BAR 16'. No one but you sees this stuff, but *everyone* hears you blow it. Don't blow it. Write on your music.

My friend Steve told me his high school choir director always said, "I need two things from you: talent, and a pencil. If I can only get one of those, I'll take the pencil."

(See #71—LAY YOUR CHARTS OUT LOGICALLY)

#13—DON'T OVERREHEARSE

WHY IT MAKES YOU MORE USEFUL:

It keeps you thinking. If you rehearse too much, you end up thinking you have it all figured out, and you stop listening critically to what you're playing and how it fits in. What you play in the rehearsal room almost never translates directly to the stage, so don't lock yourself in.

WHAT TO DO:

Make sure you know what to play, that you have a firm grasp on it, but don't memorize every note.

Let's say you're playing electric guitar on a song with a strong R&B-type feel, and your job is to reinforce the 2nd and 4th beats for most of the song, sort of higher up the fretboard to keep out of the way of the piano. You work out what you're going to play, and you make sure you have it firmly in your head. However, now that you're in front of people, you realize— the room is noisy and the bass frequencies on every instrument are being swallowed up by the carpet, people and low ceilings. Because of this, the song lacks muscle. You can help by hitting low notes on your guitar on the 1st and 3rd beats to help shore up the bottom end. Yeah, you have to be careful not to play notes that directly conflict with the other instruments, but you can at least do it wherever it works. In fact, you might even move those high notes down the fretboard a little so they're a little beefier. In other words, you're responding to the situation without sacrificing your role in the song.

THOUGHTS:

No playing situation is static. You might play the same room, the same crowd, the same songs every week, but it still changes. The people you're performing with will play slightly differently, you may have a fill-in person, or you may have never played with these people. I can't tell you how many times I've found myself onstage thinking, "Why isn't this working? It worked in rehearsal." Ask yourself *always*—is the music having the impact you thought it would? Be ready to change.

#14—SIMPLIFY.
ALWAYS SIMPLIFY

WHY IT MAKES YOU MORE USEFUL:

Simplifying brings focus. You'll play more confidently, and your music will feel better to the listener.

WHAT TO DO:

Learn what makes the song tick, what makes it move, what makes it peculiar, and then focus on ONLY those things.

Get the basic, overall *feel* of the song in your head (and body) and then stick to that feel on everything you play. If it's a 2 & 4 feel, then emphasize those hits in everything you play. If there are particular rhythmic things featured in the song, make sure you do those as well.

Are there a lot of 'big' chords, with extensions? If so, are they part of the core of the song, or something maybe added later? Strip the chords down to their basics and then keep only the big extensions if they're really necessary. Change every 9,

11, and 13 on the end of a chord to a '7'.

NO EXTRA NOTES. Play what's needed and nothing else. Ask yourself: What's the least I can play and still get the point across?

THOUGHTS:

I saw the Doobie Brothers live a few years ago. I'm familiar with all their big hits, and most of whatever else they might play. Their recordings are full of wonderful little parts, detailed things that are great to listen to. But at their concert, all that detail went out the window. They stripped their songs down to just the bare minimum—the big moves, the important, recognizable parts and *nothing else.* One of my favorites is 'South City Midnight Lady'. It's worth putting the headphones on and giving a listen. The song morphs into an instrumental section with violins, full band, and an absolutely gorgeous pedal steel guitar. They didn't have the strings with them at the concert, and the guy playing pedal steel didn't do all the exact licks from the recording. Their rendition onstage was great, but they had the good sense not to try to reproduce the recording exactly. Instead, they stuck to the main themes, the important parts, and played that simplified version beautifully. This is what you have to do when you play live. Strip the song down, play it simply and then add all the humanity and personal flair you can.

(See #63—SIMPLIFY THE CHORDS)

#15—MOVE TO AN EASIER KEY

WHY IT MAKES YOU MORE USEFUL:

You can't play effectively if you're struggling with a difficult key. Easier keys are…easier.

WHAT TO DO:

Transpose to a new key, if you can. (Of course, you'll have to convince the whole band to do this…) Find the simplest way to do this, whether that's using a program or app that does it for you, or whether it means rewriting the chord chart. Whatever you have to do, it's almost always worth it. Is the original song in Gb? Forget it. You'll limp along playing about 25% of what you could in G or F. Drop your pride and reluctance to mess with the original, and get it into a form you can work with. Offer to rewrite the chart for everyone, if they're okay with changing the key but don't know how.

Ed Schief

THOUGHTS:

I do this all the time. *All the time.* I do it because I play better in some keys than others, and I have a job to do—I have to move the audience. Nothing else matters, and certainly not my pride or some messed up sense of loyalty to a song.

As I write this, I'm sort of playing musical director for a little fundraising concert at a church. Just putting some easy charts together, making sure the band has what they need. One of the singers requested that the Eagle's 'Desperado' be moved down half a step from the original. But the original is in G, so moving in down a half step would put it in Gb. That would mean the guitar players would have to either capo and change keys (who's going to write THAT chart?) or detune their guitars for just one song. Not only that, it would slow rehearsal down-- and we only have one rehearsal. Oh—and I'd struggle along in Gb, muttering under my breath. So I texted back and suggested we move it down to F instead, which turned out to be fine. Yeah, the guitar players will gripe a little, but they'll get over it.

Come to think of it, I 'cheated' at a Christmas concert a few years ago. I was mimicking an accordion sound on the keyboard, and in the middle there was an improvised section featuring the accordion. Lots of fast-moving scale stuff. It would have been a breeze to improvise something in G, but the song was in Gb. Sheesh. So I set up a second accordion sound, using the keyboard's transpose function to move it up a half step. When the solo came around, I quick jumped to that sound and played in G. Then I switched back. I made a BIG note on the music so I wouldn't forget.

(See #17—MAKE A CAPO CHART)

#16—DON'T ASSUME THE WRITTEN MUSIC IS RIGHT

WHY IT MAKES YOU MORE USEFUL:

Catching mistakes in the music before you start saves a TON of time.

WHAT TO DO:

Listen through the piece (if you can) and match it to what you see on the page. Make a photocopy and mark on it anything that doesn't seem right to you. Bring the photocopy with you to rehearsal, along with the original, and be prepared to point out the mistakes in the chart. Be sensitive about this. Sometimes the chart is written by someone you're playing with, or the leader of your ensemble didn't catch the mistake. Be politically astute, but saving the band from an embarrassing mistake will help build trust and respect. Also remember that the others may not have seen the mistake, and will have learned it the wrong way.

THOUGHTS:

A couple of years after I left my job at The Big Church, my wife and I sat in with the band for a Sunday, two services, probably a thousand people at each service. They asked us to perform John Mayer's 'Slow Dancing In A Burning Room', so I listened carefully to what Mr. Mayer played on the recording and adapted it to what I could play confidently. I kept it close to the original. At rehearsal I was handed the chart prepared by the music director, just a words/chords chart, and it was...wrong. He had the chords just plain *wrong*. I was playing it right, and the music director (even though he wrote the chart), was playing it right on the keyboard, but I but could hear and see the bass player struggling. When I got a chance, I talked to the music director and he said, 'No, those are the right chords. I did that chart myself."

This guy had a fantastic ear, but not very much music theory knowledge, so he was *playing* it right on the keyboard, but the bass player was out in the weeds because he was reading the chart without having heard the song. So when we took a break, I rewrote the chart on a piece of blank paper. I just wrote the chords down really quick and gave the paper to the bass player. I said, "Here—these are right. Just...play these and we'll be all right." And we were. The music director never knew, and the song went well. In fact, it went *really great*! One of my favorite moments onstage.

#17—MAKE A CAPO CHART

WHY IT MAKES YOU MORE USEFUL:

It gives the guitar player (maybe you) options. If you're playing another instrument, it might move the guitar player up and out of your range, so you're not both wrestling for the same piece of sonic land. If the guitar player is inexperienced, he or she might not be able to play the chords on the music, so writing a capo chart for them might gain you a lifelong friend. It might also make the song sound a lot better.

WHAT TO DO:

I know this is extra work, and really should have been thought through by whoever's in charge, but that doesn't matter—just do what you have to to improve things. Moving the guitar player up the neck with a capo will bring the song into a guitar-friendly key, which will make their part sound better. The guitar is particularly suited to sharp keys, and most guitar players have a stable of guitar riffs they can pull out—*if* the song is E, A, D or G. Here's the rule:

For every fret they capo up, move the key down a half step. If the song is in F, rewrite it for the guitar in E, and note that they should capo up one fret. Or you could rewrite the chart in D, and instruct them to capo up three frets.

As an example:

The song you're playing is in Ab, which frankly *sucks* on the guitar, especially acoustic guitar. They'll be playing barre chords the whole time, getting hand cramps and struggling to get the strings to ring. Rewrite the chart in the key of E, and have them capo at the 4th fret, or rewrite it in the key of G and have them capo at the 1st fret. Either way, they (or you) are now ideally positioned to take advantage of all their/your cool guitar licks. Everybody wins.

THOUGHTS:

If you've never transposed a song into a different key, or written a capo chart, you have a little learning curve (remember: first time's the hardest). Do it like this:

Let's say you're moving from F to Ab. First thing you do is change every F chord in the song to Ab. Next, count up half steps (or frets) from F to Ab. It's three half-steps, or three frets. (Also, it's a minor third, for those who understand that). Take the very next chord in the song and move that one up three half steps. It might be a Bb, so change that Bb to a Db, then find every other Bb in the song and change all of those to Db's as well. It actually goes pretty quickly, and if you've never done it, you'll need to keep your instrument in your hand to help you find the pitches. Like everything in this world—do it a few times and it starts to get easier.

#18—ASK TO TALK THE SONG THROUGH BEFORE YOU PLAY IT AS A GROUP

WHY IT MAKES YOU MORE USEFUL:

It saves the band from stopping over and over because something's not clear.

WHAT TO DO:

Say this: "Before we start, can we talk through this a second?" Then make sure you know the format of verses, choruses, bridges, etc., the loud and soft sections, and anything else that can be communicated verbally.

THOUGHTS:

Oh man—I can't tell you how many rehearsals I've been

through where we launched out into a song, only to stop and say, "Wait a minute—doesn't the bridge come after the second chorus? Weren't we supposed to drop out there?" Or everyone just blasts all the way through without a thought for dynamics or how they fit into the band. Might as well not waste five minutes playing a song the way you're NOT going to play it.

Musicians can be like a dog getting his ears scratched—his back foot automatically starts thumping along. They hear a beat and they just start whacking away. If you don't get this stuff straight before you start, the default position will be for everyone to play everything all the time. Most musicians DON'T think about dynamics, they just play what they like or what feels good. Talking about it ahead of time not only saves time, it gives you a running start at playing a song with dynamics.

#19—CAPITALIZE ON THE UNPLANNED

WHY IT MAKES YOU MORE USEFUL:

It takes advantage of the moment, bringing something you could not think of ahead of time.

WHAT TO DO:

As a song unfolds with an ensemble, sometimes you hear something that rises up out of a combination of things. If you hear this, and it's cool, strengthen it. Reinforce it. As an example, a piano player might play a chord a little differently than the electric guitar player and the combination of the two sounds is just way cool. Hurray! Make sure both of them play that section strongly so the coolness is brought out. Also, see if you can figure out exactly what's cool about it, and maybe find a way to play it on yet another instrument.

Or maybe the drummer plays a part wrong once, but it's just the greatest thing you ever heard. In that case, use it!

THOUGHTS:

Another mentor for me was a guy named Rick. He was light years ahead of me. We were playing in some ensemble situation and Rick said, "Do you hear that?" I didn't. We played it again and he helped me hear that the way the guitar and keyboard were playing was sort of creating a little melody line all it's own. He sang along with it, and then I heard it. So he gave that little accidental melody line to me, and *man* it was cool.

(See #51—CAPITALIZE ON UNEXPECTED THINGS)

#20—TIE SOMETHING UNRELATED INTO MEMORIZATION

WHY IT MAKES YOU MORE USEFUL:

You'll retain more of whatever you're learning and more easily recall it when you need it.

WHAT TO DO:

Bring something into the learning process that you can tie visually or tactilely to the song. If you're cramming to learn a song you need to perform in the next few days, chew gum or suck on mints that are a very particular flavor—something you don't normally do. When you need to remember the song, put those mints in your mouth and the two experiences tied together will bring the song back more vividly.

If you're learning something to remember long term, write out a shorthand version of the song on paper, something you can bring back in your mind's eye. You might think of a better way. If you do, write me and tell me—I'm always looking for a shortcut.

THOUGHTS:

I first became aware of this during a tech-week rehearsal for a big musical. Most of the band was buried inside the set, which was large and three-dimensional, with compartments inside for most of us players. (We referred to it as the 'pants optional' setup. Okay, that was a joke, but I DID eat a lot of Peanut M&M's that week...) I could look out at the stage through a slit in the structure maybe about 10 inches high. Like I was driving a tank, or something.

During one particular song, after weeks and weeks of playing this song in the rehearsal room, I suddenly felt like something was wrong at one particular part. Like we'd hit a speed bump. Just a four bar section, or something. It didn't feel right, and I wondered if I'd missed something or was playing something wrong. I definitely felt like something had *changed,* but I couldn't put my finger on it. It happened again, same spot in the song, and it really bothered me.

The next night, during the same song, everything was fine. And then it occurred to me—every time we'd played that part of the song in rehearsal, sitting inside the set, a particular pair of women's shoes had walked by, right in front of me. I remembered them because they were nurses shoes. I didn't even know who wore them. All the movements of the cast were set in stone, so this woman walked by at precisely the same moment every time, and every time I saw the nurse's shoes I wondered who wore them. But the night before, she'd worn dark shoes and it caught my attention.

I realized I was tying a visual experience with the song, and that it was probably a BIG reason that as the tech-week rehearsals wore on, I was remembering the songs more and more easily. I was probably doing that with a lot of the visuals I got from my perch. In fact, the more I paid attention to it, the more I realized it was a pretty important part of getting all this music right.

My band played The Who's 'Can't Explain', and I found it hard to memorize at first because a couple of verses or choruses weren't the same length as the others. However, if I pictured the actual chord chart I'd written, I'd find myself thinking, "Oh yeah—we're at the bottom of the first page, where the verse is shorter..."

Just being aware of this will probably help you a lot. Conversely, if you've played a song in the same physical surroundings over and over, and then you play it somewhere else, be aware that it might not come quite as easily.

#21—LOOK OVER THE WRITTEN MUSIC AHEAD OF TIME

WHY IT MAKES YOU MORE USEFUL:

It saves you from nasty, embarrassing surprises.

WHAT TO DO:

In short, get familiar with the song and the written music as best you can. This doesn't need to be exhaustive, but the more prepared you are, the better it will go for you.

Make sure you understand the flow, check for chords or passages that might look the same at first glance, but are actually slightly different. Check for difficult chords, and if it's in an unfamiliar key, spend a little extra time with it. Make sure you can easily find your way through it. Skip this step, and you risk getting to a rehearsal (or worse, a performance) and realizing you're pretty seriously in the weeds.

And actually play the whole song through. You might *think* you have it, but you don't *know* you have it until you play it. Every once in a while you'll realize there's a chord or a passage that looked easy to play, but wasn't. It's VERY easy to skim through something and later realize you weren't really paying attention.

THOUGHTS:

This is another time-vampire at rehearsals, and the less experienced the musician, the more likely they are to think they don't need to prepare. This is because inexperienced musicians think that music works by magic.

I worked as an interim worship director one summer a couple of years ago, and I would send everyone the music ahead of time, attached as PDF's in an email. But almost nobody ever actually printed the music and brought it with them. So I started doing it myself. I made copies for everyone and brought them to rehearsal. Inside I was kind of appalled at this lack of preparation.

But one week we couldn't do a mid-week rehearsal, so in addition to the PDF's I sent a short set of written instructions for the song. I gave them the verse/chorus/bridge orders and a few other simple notes. I asked everyone to PLEASE print their own music, write on it whatever they needed to get through the song, because we needed to be up and running right away on Sunday morning. There would be no time to stop, start, answer questions, etc. On Sunday morning everyone sort of dribbled in over a twenty minute period (most of them late), and only one guy brought his own music (Anthony, if you're reading this, I LOVE YOU). The rest came in empty handed. One guy in his

30's said he 'thought his printer might be out of ink or some-thing'. *This guy owned his own business.* Instead of saving time I *wasted* time running back and forth to the copy machine as people wandered in late, empty-handed. They'd done NOTH-ING to prepare for the morning. NOTHING. They either hadn't read my email (okay...were they reading ANY of them?) or just blew it off. Yeah, I'm still a little steamed about it.

So, come on—spend a few minutes, if for no other reason than out of respect for everyone else's time.

#22—TAPE YOUR MUSIC TOGETHER

WHY IT MAKES YOU MORE USEFUL:

It keeps you from having to shuffle so much paper on a music stand.

WHAT TO DO:

This is aimed directly at church musicians who get different songs in different orders every week, but it's a good practice for anyone playing one-time gigs. Get out the Scotch Tape, lay the songs on the counter, butt them up together and run a piece of tape down the seam. Put them in two or three song chunks, whatever fits easily on a music stand. This is especially necessary if you're given something photocopied and it runs several pages. If you don't tape this kind of thing together, you end up shuffling pages the whole time you're playing. If you have to return the music, then make your own photocopies.

THOUGHTS:

I'm amazed at the number of musicians who won't take the time to do this. In fact, now that I think of it, I can't think of ONE PERSON I've ever performed with on a church stage who has done this. Well...maybe one or two. I have, however, endlessly watched bass players and guitar players furiously shuffling pages, missing parts, getting pages in the wrong order —and for some reason they just never learn. I wonder if I could get a government grant to study this aberrant behavior. Otherwise reasonable, rational, responsible adults turn into helpless third graders on a church stage.

Here's another quick tip—write numbers on the top of the page so you know which song comes first, which one second, etc. (You brought a pencil, right?) Write a '1' on the first song, a '2' on the second song, etc. Even if you have no college, you can manage this. And throw a roll of Scotch Tape in your instrument case.

#23—REWRITE THE MUSIC YOU'RE GIVEN

WHY IT MAKES YOU MORE USEFUL:

You'll very likely have something more readable, you can shorten it to one page, and you'll know the song much better for having done this.

WHAT TO DO:

Most songs are highly repetitive, at least musically. Use this to your advantage and shorten the chart. Write out only the chords to the verse, for instance, using simple lines and dashes. Try to keep them in sets of four bars. Like this:

```
|C---|- - - -|F---|----|
|C---|- - - -|G---|----|
|C---|C7---|F---|D7---|
|C---|G7---|C---|STOP|
```

If you're not singing, you don't need the words anyway, right? Do the same for the chorus, bridge, etc., and then at rehearsal notate how many of each section, the flow, etc. You'll have something useful in front of you, and something you can hold onto in case you're asked to do the song again. If you do this in software like 'OnSong', you'll be able to quickly change the key for a different situation (or quickly make a capo chart). To help keep your place, you could write the first three words or so to each section. That way if a vocalist skips around, you can find them.

THOUGHTS:

I play off and on with a drummer named Danny, and he pretty much always reduces every chart he's given to a one-pager. He always knows what's going on in a song for the obvious reason—he listened and rewrote the chart. He makes his own notes, things he'll need to remember. Whenever I walk into a rehearsal with him and see those handwritten pages, I know we're going to be okay—because the drummer has done his homework. He's almost always the most informed musician onstage.

I know this seems like a lot of extra work, but you'll get faster at it after a few tries. And really—the only question worth asking here is:

What are you willing to do to sound good and get asked back?

(See #17—MAKE A CAPO CHART)
(See #12—MAKE YOUR MUSIC EASIER TO READ)

❖ ❖ ❖

#24—PLAN TO PERFORM AT ROUGHLY 2/3 OF YOUR CAPACITY

WHY IT MAKES YOU MORE USEFUL:

You'll be far more confident, and your playing will project that confidence. You'll be relaxed onstage, you'll have energy for the whole performance and you'll make far fewer mistakes.

WHAT TO DO:

Simplify what you play, and lean into your strengths. Avoid something you already know you're going to struggle to play right. Don't sacrifice the feel of the song, but work to find a way to express what needs expressing in a way that leaves you with maneuvering room. Unexpected things will happen, and when they do you'll have a far easier time managing your playing *and* the interruption at the same time—because the song never stops.

Examples:

Change all the chords with big extensions (9, 11, 13) to 7 chords.

Don't volunteer for a big solo, or turn down the opportunity.

Play the chords or notes in the most comfortable position for you.

Play a drumbeat that you're comfortable with, rather than trying to imitate that complex beat on the recording.

THOUGHTS:

If you're sweating it out, playing right up to the edge, bad things are waiting just around the corner. Any little interruption and you're sunk, and there are ALWAYS interruptions. Also, you'll very likely project nervousness, and if you're nervous, the audience will know. They'll know, and your playing will feel tentative and weak to them. Instead of enjoying your music, the audience will spend it's attention worrying you're going to blow it. Simplify a little, and you're playing from a place of strength. If you're having fun, the audience will enjoy themselves as well.

Plus, you really don't need the aggravation of never knowing if THIS is the night you blow it. Who wants to live that way?

◆ ◆ ◆

CHAPTER 3-ONSTAGE

Performing onstage is one of my favorite places to be. It's one of the few endeavors in life that gives you instant feedback. You know immediately whether or not you're doing good, and yeah, that can be a little scary. It's the place where you learn, and very quickly, what works and what doesn't work. My friend and mentor, Joe, says, "Practicing is like studying, being onstage is like taking the test."

#25—STOP BLAMING YOUR EQUIPMENT

WHY IT MAKES YOU MORE USEFUL:

It pushes you forward. Blame your equipment and you'll stop working on your playing.

WHAT TO DO:

Don't get me wrong—play the best equipment you an afford. I do. But ask yourself this question: Would people rather hear you play Eddie Van Halen's guitar (as an example), or would they rather hear him play yours? You already know the answer. Blaming your equipment is an excuse.

Tell yourself the truth. Face the reality. Where are you weak, and what do you need to do to get better? If you don't sound like your favorite famous player, then you have to improve. To improve, you have to work at it. You have to be patient. Stop telling yourself repeatedly that you won't sound good until you get the birch drum kit, the vintage Les Paul guitar, the newest Nord keyboard or that really expensive vocal mic. Shift your focus away from the equipment and on to what goes on in your head and your hands. You probably already have adequate equipment.

THOUGHTS:

I've watched this over and over, all my life. I'll pick on guitar players because they're easy targets, but this applies to all instruments. Let's follow the thought process all the way out to the end, past the equipment excuse and into The Land Of Lying To Yourself. (I've been there several times, and it never worked out very good.)

You want to be a Rock Guitar God, the next Jimmy Hendrix. You picture yourself up on a stage, absolutely ripping through a bluesy solo, audience screaming. You invest a LOT of thought and emotional energy into this. You want it to define you. So you get a guitar, you take some lessons and you sit in your basement listening to recordings and trying to emulate them. You tell everybody how good you're going to be. You find ways to drop it into conversation. You learn how to *talk* a good guitar solo. This is going to be so great!

And then you hit a wall. This is WAY harder than it looked from the outside. Six months into it you realize—it's not going to happen right away, and it might not happen at all. You keep at it for a year, but you're STILL not anywhere near good. So instead of digging in, you tell yourself a little lie:

"I'm so limited by this crappy guitar and amp."

You need an upgrade! You research it all, and decide on a fairly expensive setup. Six months after *that*...you really don't play much better. You tell yourself another lie.

"You know, I'm just not sure Rock is my genre."

You start thinking that maybe another, different kind of music might be cooler. Hey, what about Country? So you shift your focus to country, and now THAT defines you. You buy a cowboy hat, you sell the expensive Les Paul for a loss and buy a blonde Telecaster. Vintage, $2700. You show it to your friends, you brag about it.

Yet another six months goes by and you *still* don't find yourself anywhere near where all the fun is. The only guys you can find that will even let you jam with them are...not very good. Here comes another lie:

"I need to find the right guys to play with."

Pretty soon you're telling yourself that *those* guys are a bunch of jerks.

You get the point. I worked in a music store for five or six years, and the guitar salesman bought a nice house selling guitars and amps (and pedals) to people just like that.

Look, I've done it too. It's an easy trap to fall into. Stop falling into that trap. Take the instrument you own RIGHT NOW, and start working on making yourself a useful musician. Find someone who is better than you and ask them to tell you how they do it. Stop being proud.

Musicians LOVE to help other musicians, and you should be picking brains and stealing ideas. Find a good instructor. Instead of blowing $750 on a better instrument, spend it on some instruction books and don't stop until you can do everything they show you in the book. Seriously. Don't stop.

I once pretty seriously annoyed a guy who could play the opening to the Doobie Brothers 'Minute by Minute'. I made him show it to me over and over until I thought I could remember it. Then I went home and pulled it all apart, figured out the best I could how it was put together and practiced it until I could play it. That was probably 40 years ago, and just a couple of years ago I watched a Doobies' concert video and realized that Michael MacDonald was telegraphing a 6/8 feel over what was essentially a bunch of 2/4 phrases and I started all over until I could do it like him. I made a 6/8 drumbeat on my synth and played that intro over and over. I'm not a genius, but I AM tenacious.

Tell yourself the truth and then *get busy.*

(See #76—MAKE SURE YOUR EQUIPMENT WORKS)

#26—STICK AND MOVE

WHY IT MAKES YOU MORE USEFUL:

You're complimenting the song and the arrangement, rather than stepping on toes.

WHAT TO DO:

I'm borrowing 'stick and move' from boxing. Boxers jump in, throw a punch, then drop back, moving out of the way.

The overwhelming urge of the inexperienced musician is to play more during the melody of a song, and then less in the empty spots. To move when the melody moves, then lay back when the melody slows down. This is a natural urge, but one you have to learn to turn on it's head.

The energy in a song naturally follows the melody, and in a general way it's your job to support that. But in between the notes, the words and phrases of the melody, there are always little empty spots waiting to be filled. This is where you can add something. An inexperienced player will feel the urge to play *more* when the melody gets busy, and less when it pulls back. Do that, though, and you're likely stepping all over it.

Instead, wait until the singer ends the phrase, and THERE you stick your little lick in. Like this:

Singer: 'Unforgettable, that's what you are...'

You: Do-do-DEE, do-do-DEE

Singer: 'Unforgettable, though near or far...'

You: Do-do-dee-da-do-do-DEE

You get the picture. You stick when the melody is happening, you move when it's not.

THOUGHTS:

I don't remember when, but this dawned on me one day. I realized what I was doing, but changing it was a LOT harder than I thought. I almost could NOT resist the urge to follow the energy of the melody. Once I made the mental switch, however, it got a lot easier and I found myself having fun trying to think up little things to play that would compliment the melody, or maybe even echo it a little bit. This is a VERY valuable skill. I think if you listen for this, you'll start hearing it all the time. If you don't do this, if you compete with the singer (or the instrumental soloist), the audience won't like your playing. They might not be able to put their finger on it, but they'll find your playing annoying.

#27—SET A NEW TEMPO BY SINGING IN YOUR HEAD

WHY IT MAKES YOU MORE USEFUL:

It gets you solidly into the next song with a minimum of hesitation.

WHAT TO DO:

When you're ending a song and need to get quickly into the next song, and it's your job to set the new tempo, do this:

About 8 bars from the end of the song you're playing, let go of it. Automate what you play a little, or even simplify it slightly, so that you can let go of it and start looking forward. Start singing the *chorus* of the next song. Sing it and feel it. If you're onstage and it's loud, you can even start singing it out loud. Tap your foot, slap your hand on your leg, whatever. This is, in my opinion, a BETTER way to set a new tempo than using a metronome, because it puts you inside the new song. The metronome just gives you a blinking light, and you end up sing-ing the new song in your head anyway. Sing the chorus and 99% of the time you'll set the tempo almost exactly right.

THOUGHTS:

You'll occasionally mess this up, but not very often. You might play a few bad notes at the end of a song, but that's not nearly as bad as coming in way too slow or way too fast on the next song. This works fine even if you're not pressed for time. I just sat in a church service yesterday (as I write this), and watched the piano player play the introduction to the song in 4/4, and the song was actually in 3/4. Sigh. He could have avoided this if he'd sung the song along in his head as he played the intro.

#28—BUILDING BLOCKS FIRST, SPECIFICS SECOND

WHY IT MAKES YOU MORE USEFUL:

You play the most useful part possible in every situation.

WHAT TO DO:

The building blocks of any song are the chords, the melody, the basic rhythmic moves, and the dynamics. Spend your time and energy on these things first. If you can play the big, important parts confidently, then move on to fine tuning things. Make sure the audience is hearing, for lack of a better term, *the actual song*. Give it life by paying attention to the ebb and flow of energy in the song (the dynamics), and make sure you're fitting comfortable into the whole picture. If all that is working well, and you still have time, start working on specifics. And by specifics, I'm including little instrumental parts from the recording that you think you HAVE to include. Don't spend time trying to get that right when you can't play the basic chords, or get the feel of the chorus right. It's just not as important.

THOUGHTS:

This can play out over a long time, multiple perform-ances of a song, or it can play out in the very short term, when you only run through a song a couple of times and then perform it.

I'll give you an example of how this played out for me a while back. I was playing electric guitar in a praise band, and we had very little rehearsal. At the actual midweek rehearsal, I made sure I knew what the acoustic guitar and piano were doing. I listened to them as we played the song the first time through. I also listened to how the leader wanted this song to ebb and flow—where he wanted to build it, where he wanted to pull it down quiet. I wrote those things on my music so I wouldn't have to try and remember. By the third pass at re-hearsal, I had an idea of what I wanted to play, where I could be of use. I got the important things straight in my mind. There was probably some kind of specific electric guitar part on the recording, but I ignored it.

On Sunday morning I had to get up and running on sev-eral songs, so as we played this particular song in run-through, I started choosing where I'd be on the neck (up high, down low), where I might play palm-muted power chords, where I'd play open chords and let the notes ring—that sort of thing. Then I asked myself—is this moving the song down the road better? Am I helping push the big parts, bring down the soft parts, make the song *feel* good? As we played it one last time before the first service, I felt like I had a couple of pretty good things going, made a couple more notes on the music, and called it good.

During the first service, as we performed it, I started weeding out things I didn't need to play, and keeping mental notes about what felt good and what didn't. I noticed too that the leader, singing and playing acoustic guitar, was playing a LOT harder than he did in run-through. I pulled back a tiny bit to make room. At the second service, I started feeling like I had it dialed in, and made only a few more tiny changes.

My whole purpose in this was to support the song. So on the third verse, where we'd decided to pull way, way back to just acoustic guitar, I felt like it didn't build very well as we came out of it and into the last big chorus. So at the second service I brought in palm-muted power chords about 4 bars before we moved up big into the chorus. I also remembered that the drummer didn't really push hard enough (in my opinion) at that spot, so I took responsibility for that and caught his eye, stepping nearer to him during that build-up, grinning, and using body language to sort of bring him along with me.

By the time we were done with the second service, I felt like we were actually getting pretty good at presenting that song. That's the way it goes—time is always limited.

However! If I had spent my rehearsal time trying to mimic some little thing I heard on the recording, I'd have added very little to the life and emotion of the song. Had we played that song every Sunday for 12 weeks in a row, I'd have probably gone back to the recording to see if there was anything I could make use of. There's just never enough time, is there?

#29—KEEP IN MIND THE AUDIENCE LISTENS WITH THEIR EYES

WHY IT MAKES YOU MORE USEFUL:

It helps the audience understand what they're listening to and how they're supposed to perceive it.

WHAT TO DO:

You need to do two things visually onstage: dress the part, and move with the music. Part of what you present to an audience is, for lack of a better term, a *vibe.* They really do have *no idea* how you do what you do, so they add visual cues into what they're hearing. If you look like a rocker, they'll more easily accept that you're a good rock player. Dress like a rocker on a church stage and people will think 'what's HIS problem?'. Dress like an accountant on a club stage and people will think 'He can't be all that good'. That's just the way it is.

Also, stow your cases someplace out of sight, if that's possible.

THOUGHTS:

Every once in a while, it actually pays to look sloppy. If you're playing in a rural bar, maybe that sort of laid-back, 'just put it anywhere' thing is what's called for. Look too good, they might see you as an outsider, slumming at their crummy little bar. It pays to do some research into where you're going to play. In fact, if you get the chance, go into a venue you're scheduled to play and watch another band. Spend an hour and get the vibe.

My band played a lot at a club called The White House for a couple of years. I thought we were one of the best sounding bands that played there. One night I was in Saugatuck with friends, just hanging out, and since Saugatuck is small I decided to take a walk over to The White House and see who was playing. The place was packed, the joint was jumpin'. Onstage was a four piece band. They were barefoot, ripped jeans, long hair, beads hanging from the their guitars, very sloppy looking. Maybe I'm getting old, but I thought, "That's the best you can do?" It wasn't a studied look (I think...), it looked like they'd gotten out of bed and wandered over to the club. Like they should have called their band 'Laundry Day'. And the music— it was stoner rock. Phase shifters running constantly on the guitars, they'd get a song up and running and give it what was obviously their 'treatment'. No nuance, not much in the way of dynamics, just get the boat up on plane and ride it until the song was done. I spotted someone I knew—our drummer's girlfriend, Julie. I walked over to say hi, and recognized the woman with her. I didn't know the woman's name, but I'd seen her dancing when we played. The woman turned to me and the first thing she said was, "Oh my god—this the BEST BAND that plays in Saugatuck." When Julie introduced me, the woman was a little embarrassed, but I told her she was free to like who she liked. I was, however, stunned. This band? These songs? This sound? But I couldn't deny it—the people dancing and listening LOVED THIS BAND.

As for moving with the music, I'm *terrible at it.* I smiled one night, and one of the band members said, into the mic, "Hey, Ed just smiled!". I'm sure that my onstage demeanor (or lack thereof) held us back. Thankfully, most of the rest of the band was physically demonstrative. And really, how much fun is it to watch a band onstage that just stands there? It's not *just* how you play, or *just* how you look, it's both.

◆ ◆ ◆

#30—EMBRACE BEING ONSTAGE

WHY IT MAKES YOU MORE USEFUL:

You make the audience more comfortable, your band-mates more relaxed, and the room more inviting when you're at ease in front of people. Also, you'll play better.

WHAT TO DO:

This is really about being afraid people won't like you. Here's the truth: nearly everyone watching you on wants to have a good time, and they're not looking at you critically. They WANT you to do well. They're sitting in their seat hoping it will be good. Remember—they can't do what you do. Even if you're not a terribly good musician, *they're not musicians at all.*

So remind yourself every time you walk out on a stage—this is a cool, fun, frankly wonderful place to be. Look what you're doing!

When you make mistakes, keep moving. Those mistakes

don't really matter much, and laughing at yourself onstage makes you human. Yeah, try to do your best, but remind yourself that those people out there are just like you, and they'd never DARE to get up in front.

Look—you bought an instrument, spent a LONG time learning how to play it, accepted an invitation to play, rehearsed, then you walk out onstage—but you don't want people to look at you? It's, like, *way* too late for that.

THOUGHTS:

I learned this from a guy named Dave who played at the Holiday inn. He made a big mistake, had to start over, made a joke, and kept going. I was horrified for him, but I looked around and everyone was laughing. His mistake endeared him to the audience. It made him human.

There's a local musician named Randy who I really respect. He's played onstage all his life, and now he does a solo act. Before he even gets up to play he's said hello and joked with nearly everyone in the room. He's your best friend. Yeah, he has a gift for this, but even if you don't, you could get better at it.

Have you ever had the experience of going to a concert, but not being really interested in the act? You go to see them anyway, and once you've heard them play, listened to their stories from the stage, you see them as human and you end up buying their CD on the way out. They're your new best friends! That's what's going on here—the audience wants you to be their friend, and they want to like your music.

So embrace being up front in public.

#31—SHOW UP
ON TIME

WHY IT MAKES YOU
MORE USEFUL:

Showing up on time sets you up for a successful rehearsal or performance.

WHAT TO DO:

Show up on time! Better yet, be early. This is just respectful of other people's time. If the rehearsal/performance starts at 7:00, get there at whatever time is necessary to be set up and ready to go by 6:30. If you have a lot of equipment to haul or a lot of setting up to do (multiple keyboards, or you're supplying the sound system), figure out how long it takes you to set it up, then arrive in time to do all that and still be ready 30 minutes early. When something unexpected happens (and it always does) you'll have time to deal with it.

You'll be relaxed, you'll feel ready, and you can help other people set up, run mic cables or whatever needs doing. Part of getting and keeping a playing relationship with people or institutions is being a team player and being respectful. The easier you are to work with, the more likely it is you'll get asked back.

Sometimes being late is unavoidable. In that case, you apologize profusely, beg forgiveness, promise it won't happen again (and make sure it doesn't) and set up *as fast as you can.* If you're running late and you still haven't eaten, either skip your meal or run through McDonald's and eat the food *before* you walk in the door. Under no circumstances should you show up late with a bag of food in your hand. Eat it in the car if you have to (you're already late), then hurry in the door and make your apologies. Walking in with a burger, fries and a Coke in your hand makes your apology sound like a lie.

THOUGHTS:

Consistently being late announces very loudly that your time is more important than everybody else's. Asking for special concessions at a rehearsal also sorta rots my socks. Sometimes you'll be in a situation where you have to wait at a rehearsal. Maybe you don't play on every song, maybe you have to wait twenty minutes while the some of the people work through a difficult part. Bring a book, play Angry Birds on your phone, but whatever you do, *be patient.* It's okay to ask if they'll need you right away at the beginning of a rehearsal, and if they don't, maybe show up a little later. Even so, don't interrupt a rehearsal setting up your stuff, banging in the door, etc. Better to get there early, scope out the situation, and then run to get coffee or something. Just, please, don't waste everyone's time. If you waste *my* time, I won't say anything the first time. Actually, I won't say anything the second time. I'm not everyone's dad, so I'll probably just turn down the offer to play with you again.

Sometimes bands and people will waste your time. You can walk a fine line here, just make sure you don't cross it. I worked with a bass player on a big production that ran several shows, and we had probably a dozen weekly rehearsals. Every week I'd wonder if this guy was going to show up, and every week he'd walk in, set his amp and bass down and plug in JUST in time to start. He knew we never started on time, and he was a busy guy with his own business to run and a young family. But you know what? He was never late for the downbeat of the first song. I learned to depend on him because he was always, always there when we needed him. You don't have to let people walk all over you, and if they don't respect you, maybe you should cut the cord and be done with them.

#32—SIMPLIFY YOUR MONITOR MIX

WHY IT MAKES YOU MORE USEFUL:

You keep the onstage sound cleaner, which is better for everyone. And you make friends with the sound guy—always a win.

WHAT TO DO:

When you can't hear yourself in the monitor, first ask yourself what's in the monitor that could be pulled *out*. You probably don't need to hear background singers, the electric guitar is probably *already* too loud, and you can pretty much always hear the cymbals. Just get the things you need to keep your place, then, if there's time, you can ask for little things here and there to be brought up. Doing this cleans up the stage sound considerably, eliminating extra noise.

THOUGHTS:

Here's my list for the monitor:

Kick, snare, hi hats from the drummer.
Acoustic guitar, especially if someone is fronting the band with it.
Lead singer
Myself

That's pretty much it. I really don't need anything else to keep my place and play dynamically,

I always start by saying to the monitor guy, "Take out all the electric guitars, all the background singers, and all the cymbals (except the hi hats). Also, the horn section and any other wind players." They nearly always grin back at me. They LOVE to hear this—it makes their job easier.

(See #78—EDUCATE YOURSELF ABOUT SOUND)

#33—EXPECT SURPRISES

WHY IT MAKES YOU MORE USEFUL:

You won't waste valuable time (and there's never enough time) wondering what to do when things go wrong. And they will.

WHAT TO DO:

Ask yourself what could POSSIBLY go wrong, and then figure out what you can do to be ready for it, even just mentally. Here's a short list:

—Your equipment fails.

—After you're completely set up, you're asked to move.

—You thought you'd be inside, but instead you're standing directly in the hot afternoon sun.

—You're presented with a song you've never played, and you have to play it right now.

—The father of the groom at a wedding reception asks you to play something 'really exciting, but with no vocals' as the wedding party comes in from an outside gathering you knew nothing about. (This happened to me)

—The sound guy moves your equipment without asking you, just before you go onstage. (This has also happened to me)

You get the picture. The trick is to anticipate, do your best, and then be okay with what happens. The sun will come up tomorrow.

THOUGHTS:

My band was booked for a performance at a big corporate dinner, a high-paying gig. It was about 1:30 in the afternoon and I had already loaded my equipment and was running to the store for something when my phone rang.

It was the guitar player in my band, distraught—his mother had just passed away. Like, less than an hour ago. He hated putting us in that position, but of course there was no way he could make the gig. Nobody did anything wrong, it was just one of those things.

So I raced home and started calling every guitar player I knew who could possibly fit, and none of them were available. We had to be there by 4:30 and it was already 2:00. I finally got ahold of a really good keyboard player/singer who, after being offered a LOT of money, agreed to load up his stuff and meet us at the convention center. I spent the next 90 minutes furiously printing off chord charts, assembling a ring binder, and thinking through every song in our sets, working out which ones we really couldn't do. I think I lost a year off my life that day.

How could I have possibly foreseen this? I couldn't, not specifically, but in general I could have been ready for this. I could have added another member to the band, someone like that keyboardist/singer, so that we had a larger repertoire of presentable songs and could roll with a punch like that. I could have made a ring binder ahead of time, and approached several guitar players, asking if they'd be willing to be subs.

In the end, this problem was my fault. It had actually occurred to me add someone to the band, but I thought, "Nahh, we'll be fine." I rolled the dice and lost—that company never booked us again.

#34—SERVE THE SONG FIRST, THE AUDIENCE SECOND, YOURSELF LAST

WHY IT MAKES YOU MORE USEFUL:

You'll be the most connected with the experience that you can be.

WHAT TO DO:

First, make sure you're making the most of whatever song you're playing. Make sure you're interpreting it well, playing what needs to be played, etc.

Second, make sure you're giving the audience the best experience you can give them.

Third and last, play something just for yourself. This is way, way last. Tread lightly here.

THOUGHTS:

One morning at The Big Church, there was a short skit performed by the drama dept. The scene involved a guy getting so flustered and overheated that he pulled the flowers out of a vase and dumped the water on his face. There was purposely only about a quarter inch of water in the vase. Just before the second service that morning, some of the musicians (I didn't realize they'd done this...sigh) put about an inch of ice water in the vase. The actor realized *as he was pouring the water* that he was about to get pretty wet. He went ahead and it turned out okay. I thought it was kinda funny.

Our drama director, however, was furious. She said, "What those guys just did was *disrespect the audience.* They put their own enjoyment ahead of everything else. That was a selfish, childish thing to do!"

What she said stuck with me. If you put your own enjoyment ahead of everything else, you'll quickly get a reputation for being difficult to work with, which translates into not getting asked back.

#35—EXAGGERATE DYNAMICS

WHY IT MAKES YOU MORE USEFUL:

It *sells* what your playing to the audience.

WHAT TO DO:

You have to exaggerate *everything.* You think you are, but you're not. Go overboard. Ham it up. Need to build into a big chorus? Go WAY down soft, so soft that you're practically not playing. Then build up and *explode* into the chorus. You think it'll be overkill, but I'm here to tell you:

Most of your changes in dynamics never make it past the edge of the stage.

THOUGHTS:

This is hard because it feels like you're being overly dramatic, that you're showing off. But that's only how it feels to *you*. That's not how it feels to the audience. There's an old rule for writing:

> *Tell them what you're going to tell them*
> *Tell them*
> *Tell them what you just told them*

This applies to music as well. Make everything OBVIOUS. Tiny differences go almost completely unnoticed. You'll get used to this feeling and pretty soon it won't feel so weird.

Someone said to me, way back, "Ed, you're playing all the same, all the way through." I thought, "No I'm not! I'm aware of the dynamics." It kinda ticked me off. So the next time I played, I thought, *"All right, I'll show you dynamics. It'll be a regular soap opera up there tonight."* I really hammed it up, and then started to feel a little embarrassed that I'd done it, hoping I hadn't ruined anything.

To my very great surprise, people came up to me that night and said, "Hey, you sounded great!" More than one person did this. So I started doing it more, feeling weird and exposed every time. But the more I did it, the more I exaggerated (wildly, I felt) the dynamics, the more engaging my playing became. Look—if you feel funny getting up in front of people and then 'emoting' on your instrument, maybe you should think about staying off the stage. I'm serious, because THAT'S the gig.

#36—PLAY THE
EMOTION OF THE SONG

WHY IT MAKES YOU
MORE USEFUL:

Knowing the emotion of the song (hard driving, soft, serious, tender, light-hearted, etc.) and then molding what you play to fit that basic emotion means you are linking arms with the song, rather than wrestling with it.

WHAT TO DO:

Listen. Listen and then match your tone, your rhythm, your sound to the song. Don't overthink it, just don't violate the feeling of the song.

THOUGHTS:

I gotta tell 'ya—this is something I see happening a lot. I was leading a very tender song on a church stage, with instructions to the rest of the band to gradually drop out at the end, to bring out the beautiful string parts played by a violin and cello. We practiced doing it. It sounded great. Then, during the actual performance, as I signaled to the band to fade, the drummer pushed the beat harder. *Harder.*

I thought, 'Did I miscue that somehow?', so I again gave him the 'back off' signal. I looked over my shoulder—he wasn't looking at me. He has his head down, and he was *into it,* playing louder and louder, all over the kit. Eight bars later the bass player, apparently inspired (sigh...), launched into some sort of loud, grinding triplets thingy along with the drums.

They pushed that song right into oblivion, completely abandoning the rest of us, robbing the audience of what could have been a really nice moment and putting their own fun ahead of everything and everyone else in the room. The song fell apart, the audience stopped singing, and I had a hard time even *ending* the song, they were so far into their own world. I was probably as angry and discouraged as I've ever been in a church setting.

This is such a...basic thing, but I watch people do it without thinking. They're looking for something clever to play, and not asking themselves whether it *works* or not.

Feel trumps clever every single time.

Another story: I was onstage at The Big Church I worked for, and the acoustic guitar player (a really, really nice guy, by the way) was strumming loud and firm all the way through the song. Never let up. I suggested he should pull back on the verses, but he just kept going, never letting up. Finally I turned to him and said, "Dude, you're beating that thing like a rented mule." I said it with a smile, but he *did* change his playing for the better. For years afterward, after I was gone from that job, I would run into this guy someplace and he would tell me that he was still beating his guitar like a rented mule. I might have gone too far with that...

#37—LEAVE ROOM
FOR OTHER PLAYERS

WHY IT MAKES YOU
MORE USEFUL:

The ensemble you're playing with will sound better, even if nobody realizes why. You'll also make the sound mixing easier.

WHAT TO DO:

Listen to what the other players are doing, and then find a place you fit. If the acoustic guitar is strumming 16th's, pull back to 8th's. If the electric guitar player goes high, you go low. Don't hog up the bottom end if you're not the bass player.

THOUGHTS:

This actually makes it all a lot more fun. It's *interesting* to think and play like this, and when you do, you'll find the sound of your band improves. Yeah, it'd be nice if the other players were leaving room for *you*, but in my experience this rarely, if ever, happens. Sorry to say it, but almost every musician I've played with is not thinking about the big picture, about how they fit into the ensemble. They don't listen with big ears. Better for your peace of mind and enjoyment of the moment to just let them play, and fit in around them.

#38—TELEGRAPH THE WHOLE SONG WITH YOUR INSTRUMENT

WHY IT MAKES YOU MORE USEFUL:

Doing this in rehearsal and onstage helps bring the feel, or the groove of the song alive. It makes the song jump.

WHAT TO DO:

Get the basic groove of the song into your bones—what the drums are playing, the bass, the whole overall feel, and then project that entire feel into the part you're playing on your instrument. Whatever the big, important things are in the song, project them with your instrument.

Work on this alone until you can telegraph the whole feel of the song with just your instrument. You should be able to get the basic feel of the whole thing into someone's ears all by yourself.

Start with this: listen to the drums and see if you can imitate the beat you hear. Concentrate on emphasizing the 2 & 4 beats, trying to jump in on the feeling of them

THOUGHTS:

Here's a metaphor, and maybe it will help:

Think of pieces of glass lying on the ground on a sunny day. Back up from those pieces scattered all around, and you see a single image of the sun reflected in all the pieces. Get down close and you see the *entire sun* reflected in each piece. You are one of those pieces.

Great musicians are always good at this. If you want a wonderful example of this, check out 'Dion - The Wanderer At Lunch' on YouTube. All they're doing is singing, but you can *feel* the whole thing right there in his voice and his hands. That's what I'm talkin' about!

Here's another one—'Van Halen doing their huge hit 'Panama' on just acoustic instruments. Find it on YouTube and listen. Do you hear how they manage to telegraph the whole thing, the excitement, all of it, without any of the big equipment?

In the end, you might not change the actual part you play very much to do this, but you'll project so much more feeling into the song. Remember—the part you play is part of the greater whole, and it all has to fit together. The audience isn't hearing all the parts, they're hearing the song coming at them as *one instrument.* Do your best to be a part of that instrument.

#39—DON'T WARM UP IN EVERYONE'S FACE

WHY IT MAKES YOU MORE USEFUL:

It makes you a pleasant person to be around, and adds to everyone's opinion of you.

WHAT TO DO:

Warm up at a low volume, and only enough to get yourself ready. Don't play otherwise unless you're sound checking.

THOUGHTS:

This *really* makes me grind my teeth. Someone gets their rig up and running during set up, and then they just luuuvvvv the sound of their own playing so much, they so very badly need to be heard, to show every great lick they know, to show everybody all the hip songs they know, that they crank up and play. And play, and play, and play. They play while someone else is sound checking, they play while people are trying to talk, they play so loud that everyone has to literally shout to be heard. They're completely oblivious to what everyone else is doing— it's just about them and their need to be heard and have the most fun they can.

I've done it too, and I really sorta hate myself when I realize I'm doing it. So, don't be that person. Respect the rest of the people in the room.

#40—BRING OPTIONS TO THE SONG

WHY IT MAKES YOU MORE USEFUL:

You create a higher probability the song will come off well.

WHAT TO DO:

Listen to the song in your head and imagine what it will sound like given the players you'll be working with. A really busy acoustic strumming part might be just the thing to bring, but only if the rest of the band can support it and leave room for it. If you know the players, you might already know how it will go, and if you don't know them, you really don't know the answer at all. You need options.

There might be a really great bass part that you've either copied from the recording, or that you thought up yourself, but if the drummer can't lock in with it, you're wasting your time and inviting frustration. Bring the cool thing you can do, but have a couple of other approaches in your back pocket.

Examples:

Drums: Bring that funky beat with the little anticipated accents, but have a solid, good-feeling 2 & 4 beat you know will work as well.

Bass: A bass line that weaves and moves through the song, covering not only root tones but utilizing thirds and fifths as well—that might be great, but be ready with a simpler approach using more root tones and less movement.

Acoustic Guitar: Bring a capo chart (I talk about this elsewhere) so you can pull out various licks and tricks you know in various keys. Work something out that plays farther up the neck as well. It might be cool for one verse or one chorus. You could even snap a capo on quick for one verse and play something interesting, pulling it off again for the rest of the song.

Electric Guitar: Keep that chugging palm-muted part ready, but find a place on the neck you can play longer tones in case that doesn't fit.

Keys: Be ready to play in the middle of the piano (a full, strong sound), but bring little arpeggios you can play an octave higher in case the guitars fill up the middle and leave you no room.

Everybody: Definitely steal cool ideas from the recording. Just don't marry them.

THOUGHTS:

The song you're attempting with a group of people will

likely go together only one or two ways. Most players are just not terribly versatile, so they're probably going to play what they're going to play. They'll have something they do that's strong, but when they do that, it might change the way the rest of the band has to play.

At The Big Church, I had a drummer with really, really good hands, but he could only play whatever just...came out of his hands. He couldn't stick to a kick drum pattern, or any pattern for that matter. He never played anything quite the same way twice. But what he *could* play was usually pretty good. So at Wednesday night rehearsals I would have a couple of things in mind, and then I'd say, "Let's just play this song through one time to get used to it." (I didn't always do that, but with this guy, I needed to) While we were playing, I'd listen to his drum part. Usually what he played the first time was basically what I was gonna get. After that first run through I'd start pointing the other instruments in a direction that worked with the drums.

Had everybody played what was on the recording, that might not have worked with the drum part he brought to the song. I'm not sure anyone was aware I was doing this, but doing it always made the songs work better. In this case I was bringing the options *for* the other players, but the effect was the same.

#41—FIGURE OUT THE OTHER PLAYERS

WHY IT MAKES YOU MORE USEFUL:

You can play something that complements them, rather than fight over sonic territory.

WHAT TO DO:

Watch and listen to the people you play with. Figure out their strengths and weaknesses, what they're likely to do in a particular situation, what trips them up every time, etc. Use that information to figure out what you can play to make the song impactful, the mood lighter, the ensemble playing better together.

Let's say you have a bass player who is rock solid, but struggles with slapping and popping—that super rhythmic thing the R&B players do. Still, your band wants to play a song that sort of leans on that bass style. You can anticipate that he or she will struggle, will feel bad, or maybe be embarrassed and defensive. They may say the song is not a good choice for the band for reasons *other* than the bass part. You also know that the guitar player has really fast hands and a strong sense of rhythm. You say, "I have an idea. Let's make the guitar really funky, add a little hi hat thingy along with it, and make it a little different than the original recording."

THOUGHTS:

At The Big Church we had a high school drummer who laid down maybe the most rock solid 2 & 4 I've ever heard. He'd hit the snare head and the rim at the same time—a rimshot—and it would sound like a rifle crack. It was huge, it was awesome, it made everything we did *so* funky and solid. As long as it was in 4/4 time. He couldn't play any other beat. 3/4 time stumped him, so did 6/8, so did swing. He just really couldn't play those things. With him, it was boom, whack, boom-boom whack.

When our service-planning team would meet and discuss songs, I'd always look to see who was playing that week. If it was this guy, I'd subtly (or maybe not so subtly) move us in the direction of 4/4 songs. Then for the prelude and offering songs (always my choice) I'd pick plain old rock and roll songs.

After I left that job I came back one Sunday to play in the band. The guy who took over for me was, to put it mildly, *extremely* talented. But...we had that same high school kid playing drums that morning and one of the songs had a tricky drum opening on the original recording.

My talented successor was bent on opening the song with that tricky drum part. Every time we started that song during Sunday morning run-through (I was called last minute and didn't make Wednesday rehearsal) NONE of us could hear where to come in. None of us could count along with him. I asked the leader to count in so I could hear where the downbeat was, but even then I couldn't hear it. Over and over we tried, and every time the leader got more and more frustrated. When I got a chance I pulled him aside and said, "What are you doing? Just cut that drum opening. Jeez. You're beating the crap out of us and humiliating the drummer. It's NOT going to work." (I'd known this talented director since he was a kid, and he worked under me as an intern, so I could push him a little.)

This was during a very, very busy Sunday rehearsal that included lights, a million mics, a drama to run through—we didn't have time. When you're in that situation, think about the weaknesses of your players and work around them. Think of the strengths of your players and lean on them.

#42—ONLY PLAY NOTES THAT MAKE MONEY

WHY IT MAKES YOU MORE USEFUL:

Playing simply and sparingly sounds better, leaves more room for other musicians and makes the sound person's job easier.

WHAT TO DO:

Ask yourself: What's the least number of notes/strums/hits I can play and still make my part work? Reduce—always reduce. If the feel of the song has 16th's, you don't have to play every one of them. Play 8th's, and then throw in the occasional 16th. Doing that gives the feel of 16th's without the messiness. Inside the part you're currently playing will be a set of notes that are actually the core of it all. Think, listen, then get rid of everything else. *Play clean.* Seriously. If you've never thought about this, I can pretty much guarantee you're in the habit of overplaying.

THOUGHTS:

A friend of mine went to LA and hung out with some big time studio guys. He asked a professional arranger for advice, and the guy said, "Only write notes that make money."

In the world of playing onstage, let that be your motto— you only play notes that make money.

George Bernard Shaw said this, and I think it applies:

"A fool-proof method for sculpting an elephant: first, get a huge block of marble; then you chip away everything that doesn't look like an elephant."

Find the notes that are the essence of the part, and only play those. What a difference it makes when you listen to a band that understands this.

#43—READ BODY LANGUAGE

WHY IT MAKES YOU MORE USEFUL:

You'll know things you need to know without having to ask.

WHAT TO DO:

Watch for visual cues from the other people onstage. Their body language will often tell you all you need to know. Are you uncertain whether THIS is the big chorus? Watch the drummer—he'll be leaning into the kit, preparing to launch a big fill to bring in the chorus. Are we at the end of the song? If the singer puts her mic down and steps back, that's a great clue.

Is the guitar player remembering he's supposed to play a solo in this next part? If he's looking down and stomping pedals, he's probably getting ready for it. If he's staring at a girl in the audience, he might need reminding. Are we doing one more chorus? If the singer is taking a step forward and taking a deep breath, the answer is yes.

You get the idea.

THOUGHTS:

I do this constantly to help keep my place onstage. I played in a praise band led by a guy who played guitar and sang. He always wanted to modulate up a step to 'take the song to the next level'. I just didn't know *when*. So I'd watch his head. He'd play along without looking at the guitar neck most of the time. But when we were getting ready to move to a new key, he's ALWAYS look down at the neck to make sure he had the new position. This would happen in maybe the last two bars before the change. So every time we came to the end of a section, I'd look up and watch his head. This never failed.

#44—STOP BEING CLEVER

WHY IT MAKES YOU MORE USEFUL:

The parts you play will fit better. Also, you'll be easier to work with.

WHAT TO DO:

Dole out your clever stuff very, very sparingly. You're not the smartest person in the band, you're not the cleverest, and nobody cares about all the cool licks. Sorry to ruin your fun, but play what *fits*. Play what the song needs, what makes the song better. If you can do that AND be clever, well, take the occasional shot. Congregations don't care about clever, dancers don't care about clever—they just want something that moves them.

THOUGHTS:

I have played some really clever stuff onstage at clubs or churches, and watched as *nobody noticed.* My dance band would work hard at something really great, really hard to play, and then watch everyone head to the restroom, talk amongst themselves, order more drinks, etc.

Working hard to be clever will make you hard to work with, because the core of it is your *own* enjoyment, and not that of the listeners.

Jazz is different. There, you can clever it up so much that everyone (including you) forgets what song you're playing. You'll also be playing to about 15 people and getting paid enough money to cover gas and pizza. In other words, it might be cool, but it's not *useful.*

#45—MAKE FRIENDS
WITH THE AUDIENCE

WHY IT MAKES YOU
MORE USEFUL:

It connects you with the people you have been hired to please.

WHAT TO DO:

You're working from the time you show up to a venue until the time you get in your car and drive away. Every contact you have with people in this circumstance is part of what you're offering. See them as your friends. See them as people who've come to have a good time--provided by you. Talk to them before, after and during. They *want* to like you, and they want a piece of you. They don't know how you do what you do, but watching you do it makes them want to be your friend. So be their friend. Talk to them during breaks, talk to them from the stage like they're your friends. Talk to them while you're packing up at the end of the night.

THOUGHTS:

I have been on stages all my life, and *still,* when I'm watching a band I think,

'*They're so cool. Those instruments are so cool. I want to hang out with them, be recognized by them. I want to be part of their crowd.*'

Invite people to be a part of your circle and you've gained a fan--and everybody anywhere near your gig is the audience.

My friend Roland, who played guitar in my band, said one night, "Let's start splitting our tips with the servers, or whoever it is that took care of our food and drinks tonight. It'll build a good relationship." That was SUCH a good idea. We did it every time after that, and it was instrumental in getting us asked back a few places. Make friends everywhere you go.

If you see the audience as the enemy, it's an indication that you see yourself as a misunderstood artist. Maybe you are, but a misunderstood artist *isn't useful.* Useful musicians get paid and get asked back. Misunderstood artists are lonely and broke.

Remember—you're in the service industry. You may think you can have it both ways, but I'm telling you—that's not likely. At least, almost no one sees you as an artist. You're providing a service when you perform. Go ahead and be an artist, but don't expect to get paid for being one.

Here's an example from one of the most popular musicals acts of all time—The Beach Boys. My daughter and I went to see them at, of all places, a high school gym. In the middle of the afternoon on a Saturday. No light show, just the band on a collapsible stage and people sitting in the bleachers and on folding chairs. They played a GREAT show, and at the end, Mike Love, that famous voice, invited people up to stand around the stage.

There were probably 150 people, mostly older women, crowded up around the front of the stage. Mr. Love, Sharpie in hand, signed album cover after album cover while he sang a medley of the old hot rod songs. When they'd played their last song, as the crew started stripping the stage, Love sat on the edge and talked and signed until—ready for this?—*there was no one left who wanted to talk with him.*

I was so impressed. This guy has had a 50 year career, has nothing to prove, and is a legend. And yet there he was, chatting with people, thanking them for coming out, giving them a piece of himself. How many times do you suppose he's done that? My guess: every single time. He makes friends with every audience he stands in front of.

#46—PLAY CONFIDENTLY

WHY IT MAKES YOU MORE USEFUL:

Confident playing covers over a multitude of sins, and it just plain sounds better than tentative playing. Confident playing draws the audience in.

WHAT TO DO:

Play boldly. Play like you just KNOW you're doing it right. Even if you're not. When you play like this, you'll pull everyone up with you. The song feels better, the parts work together better and the audience relaxes. Be ready to change if you're wrong, but always project your part strongly, confidently. Even in quiet, delicate parts—play them with authority.

THOUGHTS:

My friend and mentor Rick use to say, 'Give it a whack and wish it well'. I used to say to the people in my Big Church bands, 'Play it wrong, play it loud'. They gave me a hard time about it at first, but I think a lot of them took it to heart, and we sounded pretty good a lot of the time.

One weekend at The Big Church we did a particular song as a performance number, with a soloist named Candice who frequently sang as a guest. It was a full band number, and toward the end of the song we modulated up a full step. We were doing three services on a Sunday at the time, so by the time we got to the third service it was easy to lose concentration. And I did.

As we approached that spot, I took my eyes off the music. I don't remember why, but I was probably thinking about lunch. And then something was wrong. Something was *not right.* This all happened pretty fast, but in the space of about two bars I realized—some of the players were *in the wrong spot on the music.*

I had a flash of annoyance, but that passed quickly because I realized...it was me. I'd lost concentration and jumped four bars ahead--into the new key. It was *me.* But I was SO in the habit of playing confidently that *everyone else thought they were wrong.* They all jumped up four bars to match *me*, instead of playing it right. It was like the whole band hit a speed bump doing 60mph. We landed without crashing, Candice found us, and we finished okay. It was almost a train wreck.

I apologized to everyone afterward, and in the spirit of Christian love, they beat the tar out of me for it. But Candice had left for the day because she had nothing more to sing and it was the last service. A month later she showed up again to sing with us, and backstage I pulled her aside.

"Hey Candice—sorry for what happened on that Rebecca St. James song."

She said, "What do you mean?"

I said, "The third service, that trouble we had—that was my fault. I jumped four bars."

Without hesitating she hit me in the arm so hard that I thought my nose was going to bleed. I was checking my teeth for loose fillings.

I said, "OW!"

She said, *"That's for letting me go a whole month thinking it was MY FAULT."*

I should have kept my mouth shut. I think I may have a small reputation for being a player that never makes mistakes, but in part it's because I always LOOK like I'm not making mistakes.

A technical note:

This is especially important when you play dissonant notes. So in a Cma7 chord, the notes are C, E, G, B. A very dissonant and striking way of arranging those notes would be to put the C and B right next to each other, voicing the chord as G, B, C, E. Played tentatively, it could sound like you're playing a wrong note. Played confidently, but softly, it has a delicate, bright, even brittle sound. Played confidently and loudly, it really makes a statement. And if the two notes that clash in that chord are given one each to different instruments, you'd better play your half of that little interval with lots of *conviction* or it will sound like you're flubbing it.

#47—BE SENSITIVE TO OTHER PLAYERS' SHORTCOMINGS

WHY IT MAKES YOU MORE USEFUL:

You create good will. You get asked back.

WHAT TO DO:

Watch and listen. Keep an eye out for a player or singer who's struggling, and see what you can do to help them. Do it quietly if you can, without anyone seeing. Remember that a musicians' identity is often wrapped up in their ability to play or sing—so instead of knocking that down to make yourself look better, see if you can improve it.

THOUGHTS:

I was a young player in a recording studio session and struggling for something useful to play on a particular track.

Rick (I've mentioned him elsewhere) came over and said, "Hey Ed—play this". And then he showed me the coolest, funkiest figure to play that involved little ghost notes with my left hand. It wasn't hard, and I picked it up right away. This was during a break in the action, so nobody really saw. When we picked it up again and started recording, I played what he'd shown me. It sounded cool.

Standing a few minutes later in the mixing booth, listening to the playback, one of the singers said, "Did you hear what Eddie played there? Ed, you've been holding back on us!" I started to say something but Rick jumped in and said, "Ed's got the moves, man." He didn't even take credit for it. I was *very* loyal to Rick for that, and for other things like it.

And now here's how NOT to do this...

There was a young woman, a college student, who sang with us sometimes at The Big Church. She was a good singer, but suffered from horrible stage fright. We sat backstage one week, waiting for the sermon to end so we could go out and do our last song—on which she was singing lead. I was sitting next to her and stage fright was all over her. As God is my witness, I tried to help her get over it.

In an effort to lighten her up, in an effort to help her see that all this was just not worth all the worry, I said, "Hey Sarah— that song you're going to sing in a minute? It's SO IMPORTANT. I mean, we rent this building, we invite the public, we plan these services, we rehearse, and then the pastor preaches, and then, at the end, the WHOLE THING is brought home by the song we're playing. EVERYTHING in this service hinges on it being perfect. I mean, people might actually leave and never find God if you mess up even one little note."

I thought surely she'd laugh and see that the exact opposite of what I was saying was true, that our little part in the service was just that—one little part.

Sarah didn't take it that way. She almost threw up. When I saw what was happening I tried to explain myself, but it was time to go out onstage. She did okay, but I was read the riot act by several people. I wrote her a letter, explaining and apologizing, but I'm pretty sure that was the last time she ever sang with us. Several years later I ran into her, married, kids running around her, and I went up to her and apologized one more time. I was hoping she didn't slap me. Instead...ready for this?...she didn't remember it.

#48—DON'T LOSE CONCENTRATION DURING REPEATED PERFORMANCES

WHY IT MAKES YOU MORE USEFUL:

Consistent playing on the same song over and over makes you reliable.

WHAT TO DO:

Be aware that repeated performances of the same song will dull your senses and make you forget things, lose your place, or just plain play dispassionately. Remember that the audience is probably hearing the song for the first time—you owe it to them to play it well. If you've identified someplace in the song you tend to slip up, mark that spot on the music. If you're getting sleepy between performances, drink coffee, go for a walk outside, do some pushups, eat something spicy—find something that will give you renewed energy. You have to discipline yourself to play with passion and energy every single time you go up onstage, no matter how sick of it your are. You're a *performer*.

THOUGHTS:

At The Big Church we used to call this 'Second Service Syndrome'. We'd rehearse on Wednesday, run through everything on Sunday morning, and the first service would go great. Second service, we'd relax, we'd think, "Hey, we got this!", and then flub something out of overconfidence. Third service...we'd start forgetting things wholesale because we were tired. I almost always said something on the way out to repeat a service, reminding everyone to be on their toes. In fact, I'd keep an eye on people during the performances, watching for a lapse of attention, giving people visual cues for important parts.

I lost concentration once at a Big Christmas Program, and even though it was only one performance, it came after a long, grueling day of rehearsing.

It was the big Christmas program, and the People Who Decide These Things had scheduled an entire evening of music, probably twenty songs, interspersed with readings. I thought it was way, way too much. The music for these choral-type songs came from those choir books with piano and four-part vocals all on one page, so you got maybe four measures per page, and sometimes only two. These arrangements would run ten, fifteen, even twenty pages. I was working part time at that point, so I literally didn't have time to rewrite all the songs into handy words-and-chords charts. I just photocopied everything. A million pages. I taped each song into roughly five page chunks for myself, and when I was done with each chunk, I'd pull it off the piano and throw it on the floor. Twenty songs times three or four long, taped-together chunks—it was a stack about an inch and a half thick. And every time we'd rehearse, I'd have to pick them up off the floor and reorder them. It was making me cranky.

About half way through the Big Christmas Program, a trio of elementary-aged kids got up on stools and did a reading. They'd read, we'd play a song, they'd read some more—it required paying close attention so I could bring the band in and out. My mind wandered. I'd been at church since 6:30 that morning for the two morning services, then rehearsed all afternoon, and now it was Sunday evening.

There was an offering song (instrumental, just the band) and then back to the kids. And then...there was dead air. Nobody was reading, nobody was taking. I thought, "Okay, here we go. One of those kids forgot their part, can't find their place, and now we have an embarrassing silence onstage. THIS is what happens when you over-program a service. Now one of those kids is going to go home crying and have a bad Christmas memory the rest of his or her life."

I was really getting steamed, thinking about what I was going to say at the next staff meeting, picturing one of the kids twenty years later, sobbing out their tale of Christmas woe on a psychiatrist's couch, when one of the singers turned toward me a little and said, "Let's all sing that old Christmas favorite, O Come All Ye Faithful". I thought, "Well, don't look at ME, sister."

But then a thought—like a dinosaur being bitten on the tail and the nerve impulse taking three minutes to travel to its brain—crept in. Hadn't we just played 'O Come All Ye Faithful'? We had. We'd done it for the offertory! And then in a rush I realized what had happened. In an effort to save time, I'd used that song as the offering song, saving myself the time and effort of coming up with yet *another* song to rehearse. I'd even congratulated myself on being clever. We'd play it as an offering song, then there'd be a reading, then we'd sing the song. Clever, I thought. Except...as we played it during the offering, I threw the music on the floor. And now I needed that music.

There I sat, everyone waiting for me to start the song, and the music was in a pile of papers on the floor next to the piano bench. I had no choice but to lean over, search through the pile, find the multi-page, taped-together sheets, and replace them on the music rack in reverse order. It was a humiliating one-man show, made worse by the knowledge that I'd just spent 30 seconds thinking bad thoughts about everyone connected with this.

So, you know, don't lose your concentration onstage or *you'll* be the one lying on a psychiatrists' couch.

#49—THINK OF THE ACOUSTIC GUITAR AS PERCUSSION INSTRUMENT THAT PLAYS NOTES

WHY IT MAKES YOU MORE USEFUL:

Being aware that the acoustic guitar generates a lot of high frequency pick noise means you can use it to firm up the percussion section.

WHAT TO DO:

If the drummer or someone else is having trouble staying with the band because they can't hear everyone, turn the acoustic guitar up in their monitor. They'll hear those high 'scratching' sounds from the pick on the strings, and it will help them keep their place.

If there's not much for the acoustic guitar to do on a song, have the guitarist mute the strings with their left hand and strum something rhythmic on those muted strings. This works great.

If the song you're performing needs a little extra percussion help, turn up the highs on the acoustic guitar so the audience hears the pick sound more.

If the song breaks down to just drums, strum the muted strings along with the drums for a bigger sound.

THOUGHTS:

I honestly never thought of the acoustic guitar this way until a couple of years ago, playing as a guest at a church service. The drummer (who I knew) said, "You're playing acoustic? Great! I have trouble hearing on this stage and your strumming will act like a shaker."

#50—SET UP SO YOU CAN SEE EVERYBODY

WHY IT MAKES YOU MORE USEFUL:

You can communicate non-verbally with your fellow players, and you listen better when you're watching.

WHAT TO DO:

Ever notice how much easier it is to understand somebody in a noisy room when you're watching their lips? It's the same with live music. You'll just plain hear better. Also, you can give and take cues, often communicating with only a nod or a little body language.

Rock your body back and forth to communicate the tempo or a change in the feel. Grin at somebody who's playing something really great. Signal that it's YOUR turn to take a solo. Signal the end of the song.

You can also anticipate what someone is going to do. When a musician enters into a new section, a new feel, whatever, they often signal it with their body. Key change coming up? Watch the guitar player to see if he looks down at the guitar neck to get his place right. Does the singer think the song is too slow? Watch for her to stamp her foot or move more, trying to pick up energy.

Whenever you can, set yourself up with good sight lines. You need to see all the other musicians onstage, to start with. I like to see the drummers, because a lot of cues come from them. If you're unsure whether this is the big chorus coming up, watch the drummer—they'll adjust in their seat and lean into a big drum fill. The leader/singer/soloist is next, because they're calling the shots onstage, and after that, anybody else I'll regularly interact with.

If I can, I also want a good view of the audience so I can read the room.

THOUGHTS:

I used to play behind a worship leader that had only one signal—he'd wave his hand around in circles behind his back. I'd think, 'Well...we're nowhere near the end of the song, so we're not ending....it's plenty fast, so he doesn't want it to speed it up...he DOES love to change keys, always modulating up to give the song more energy, and since he's playing guitar he'll want a sharp key, and since we're in D right now, he'd move to E, and now he's waving his hand behind his back...now he's looking down at his left hand, a sure sign he's moving his hand to a different position...annnnd here we go!'.

Everything you see is information you can use. Is the guitar player leaning down to turn up his amp? (Probably) This might lead to the escalating-stage-volume monster rearing it's head, but better to know it ahead of time. Does the piano player have a solo or something important to play, and are they remembering? If they're reaching for coffee, maybe not. Maybe you should be ready with something to fill in. Are you too loud? Is someone trying to get your attention? A very long list of things can happen onstage that aren't planned, and the sooner you see them coming, the better prepared you can be. Watching another player onstage really throwing themselves into a song can revive you when you're feeling lackluster.

The very last thing you want onstage is to feel isolated. It drags down your ensemble playing, to start with, and it robs everyone (audience included) of the chance to interact with you.

#51—APPOINT SOMEONE TO MAKE DECISIONS ONSTAGE

WHY IT MAKES YOU MORE USEFUL:

It avoids confusion.

WHAT TO DO:

Either lead or follow, but put somebody in charge of making quick decisions onstage. When the unexpected comes, let one person make the decision. You can always second-guess them later.

THOUGHTS:

The first time I heard the band at Saddleback Community Church in Lake Forest, CA, they blew me away. They were having *fun*. On one song the song leader invited the sax player out to take a solo. I assumed this was planned ahead of time, which is fine. He blew a *fantastic* solo. (I thought 'where did they *find* this guy?' But of course, it was a huge church—20,000 attendees on a weekend—and this *was* Southern California.) As the solo was ending, the song leader turned to the sax player and said, "Do it again!". I held my breath. I thought, 'If that request was pre-planned to LOOK spontaneous, I'm going to be grievously disappointed.'

So I looked at the band to see how they acted. Were they surprised? Did they see it coming? I assumed the piano player was the leader, so I watched. To my everlasting delight, everyone in the band, when they heard 'Do it again!', looked at the piano player. The piano player put his hand up in the air and made a little circle—'Take it around again'. I think I laughed out loud with delight. This was wonderful ensemble playing. It was soooo refreshing to see in a church band. There was a hierarchy in place: the song leader called for a second solo, and the band looked to their leader to confirm it.

And then they *just rolled with it.* I wanted to run up there and...I don't know...JOIN them. Their music was so *fun.* It was real. It was human. It was compelling. It was not just live music, it was *a*-live music. They didn't know the extra solo was coming, but they followed the leaders and made great music out of it.

Later, in a breakout session with the band leader—his name was Bob Barrett—he said, "Spontaneity and improvisation are two pillars of live playing". Just writing this, 22 years later, I remember how *badly* I wanted to play with those guys.

#52—DON'T SLAVISHLY COPY THE ORIGINAL RECORDING

WHY IT MAKES YOU MORE USEFUL:

It opens you up to playing the best possible version of the song *right now*—for the players you're with, for the people who are listening, for size of the room and for the moment. It frees you up to play something that actually works.

WHAT TO DO:

Strip the song down to it's core—the melody, the chords, the basic feel and any instrumental parts that are tied strongly to the song. Then build it back up the way that works best *right now*. Simplify it if you need to, change it into a key that works better for everybody, drop the 47 repetitions of the chorus on the original or ADD 47 repetitions if that makes sense. Whatever you do, make it work RIGHT NOW.

Think of the basic direction of the song, then (this bears

repeating) make it work with *your* players, for *your* audience, in *that* room. Play what works *today.*

Be an interpreter, not an imitator.

If you can get this done quickly, then by all means—dip into the original recording and see if there are cool things you can add back. Just don't *start* with those cool little things and neglect the big, important things. You'll waste your time and play the song weakly.

THOUGHTS:

I know what you're thinking: "Yeah, but who am I to alter the original recording?" I'll tell you who you are: You're the person who has to answer for how your music sounds. You're the one standing up in front of an audience and taking a chance. So take control.

In a rehearsal one week at The Big Church, somebody said to me, "Hold on. We can't do this song! *We don't have a flute player.*" There was a flute solo in the song, and to that person, well, that was how the song *went.* I realized that these wonderful people, many of whom I still consider friends, were stuck thinking the song was the song was the song.

I said, "Yeah, but we have a guitar player who can take a solo. Let's just do that instead." I got blank looks at first. This was a brand new thought for them. It took me a couple of years, probably, to help them all see that the song—any song—was just a set of chords, melody and maybe a few other things. The rest of it was how somebody else, other than us, chose to *express* the song. Big difference.

The Music Police are not in the audience, and besides—you probably shouldn't play whatever part is on the recording, at least not exactly. You probably...well, you probably *can't.* And if you *can,* the rest of your band might not be able to perfectly imitate *their* parts, and then that cool part you learned might not work right. You should at least be ready to alter it.

The people who played on the recording are not onstage with you. Remember—that song was recorded by *really* good players in a perfect recording environment where they had complete control of the sound and could stop and start. And they only had to get it right once. That's NOT your situation. At all.

The drummer on your stage plays the groove a little different. The recording has an electric guitar, but the guitar player on your stage is playing an acoustic, and so forth. The music goes together differently every time. You have to adjust on the fly. For instance: the guitar on the original recording is playing a funky little figure way up the neck on the electric, but the guitarist onstage with you is playing an acoustic guitar, and is strumming open chords. If you're on piano, you need to move up and out of the acoustic player's range so the two of you aren't circling around middle C and making it muddy. Or better yet—anticipate this, rewrite the chart for the acoustic player so he/she can capo up the neck and get out of your way.

Play the room.

#53—MOVE UP AND DOWN TO STAY OUT OF A SINGERS' RANGE

WHY IT MAKES YOU MORE USEFUL:

Your accompaniment will sound much better behind the soloist.

WHAT TO DO:

Play just above or just below their vocal range to keep the notes you're playing from competing with the notes they're singing. A high note for most men is around an E above middle C. For women, it's an octave higher. It will move around a little from person to person and from one key to another, but this should put you in the ballpark.

Above or below, doesn't matter, and you can get close—just don't sit right in the middle of their range the whole time. Once in a while this is a rule you can break, but be careful with it. This also makes the sound person's job easier—they don't have to work at bringing the voice up to the front of the mix. (When several instruments/voices occupy the exact same range, the sound engineer has to fiddle with the EQ settings to get the most important one to pop out.)

THOUGHTS:

I don't have much to add here, other than to be patient with yourself. If you're not much of an improvisor, and you're reading from the music, at least try to move your right hand part up or down an octave to meet the need.

#54—PLAY THE ROOM

WHY IT MAKES YOU
MORE USEFUL:

Being aware of the space you're playing in and adjusting to the situation means you're making the very most of every circumstance. It makes the music you present feel more *real.*

WHAT TO DO:

Everything about your performance should fit the room. Your equipment should fit the size of the room. Your volume should fit the size of the room. The part you play. All of it should take into account the size of the room, the size of the audience, and most of all, the people for whom you're playing. Make what you play *fit the situation.*

THOUGHTS:

Scott is one of my favorite local drummers. He's an *interesting* drummer. He's familiar with a wide variety of styles, listens constantly to a wide variety of music, and then...here it comes...he shapes his drum part *for that room, for that song, for those players, for that audience.* He played sometimes at a little church I attended. Small, low ceilinged room, 125 people max. The stage was right up to the front row, and wasn't really a stage —just a platform about 4 inches high.

He'd bring a kick drum, snare and hi hats, and that's it. He knew it was all he needed.

I watched Scott play (my wife: "Ed, what are you THINK-ING about?") one day. He was watching the leader and the other players, and I could *see* him thinking. Was the leader pushing for a little more energy on the second verse? Scott helped him take it there with a little more volume, a little change of stick position on the snare. The bass player would play something, Scott would pick up on it and reinforce it. For a change of pace, I saw him play his right hand on the rim of the snare instead of the hi hats.

And here's maybe the coolest thing: his playing *disappeared into the song.* I saw him doing all these little things, but the congregation didn't. And that's exactly right. Scott *served the song,* and by doing so, served the congregation. And he did it gladly, and with a tiny, curious little grin on his face.

He wasn't thinking 'Watch this', but rather "Oh, you know what would be cool?"

And to be clear: Scott can play some really cool stuff. If there's room, he always includes it in his performance. He just doesn't put his own fun first. Or maybe he does. Maybe he defines fun as making the song really cool.

I have probably thirty years more experience, but I've learned from watching Scott play.

Serve the song, serve the listener, serve yourself--in that order.

#55—PLAY IT IN YOUR OWN VOICE

WHY IT MAKES YOU MORE USEFUL:

It makes you unique. Nobody else does it quite like you do, and that means if someone wants what you do, they need *you*.

WHAT TO DO:

There will be a natural way things come out of you, even if you're reading music note for note. It's the sound of your fingers on the strings, the keys, handling the sticks, your embouchure on a horn—there will always be things that make you slightly unique. Find those things and don't be afraid to let them out.

When you're interpreting music (playing off a chord chart, improvising), you'll need to perform certain tasks—but perform them the way you sound best, within the bounds you're allowed.

Always ask yourself what you need to do to get your specific job done, and then do it the way you think it sounds best. Imitating is good if you don't know your way, but soon enough you should be developing a style. Find your strengths and exploit them. Do you have a particularly strong fingerpicking style on the guitar? Use that as much as you can. Do you have a particular drum style that has come to work well for you? Do it.

THOUGHTS:

Don't be afraid to say, "I think it's better this way".

#56—PLAY IN THE MOMENT

WHY IT MAKES YOU MORE USEFUL:

This sets you up to play the best possible music you can, right now, right here on this stage, with these people, for these people.

WHAT TO DO:

Always, always, always keep your eyes and ears open. Read the people around you and be ready to adapt. Listen to what you're playing through your listener's ears, and ask yourself if what you're playing *right now* is the best thing to play for *right now*. Most of all, enjoy the musical moment you're in! Find something to enjoy as the music goes by, and then...enjoy it. It might be a drummer laying down a far funkier groove than he ever has, it might a singer spontaneously reaching up for a note she's never hit before.

THOUGHTS:

I've read that battle plans usually never survive the first two minutes of actual shooting. It's this way onstage. Things change. In rehearsal you decided to make the last verse soft and meditative, but when people fill up the seats in the auditorium, that soft verse doesn't even make it off the stage. You don't know this until that last verse starts, and you realize there's a crying baby, a car horn honking in the parking lot, traffic noise, people singing along—whatever. When you hear this, you change. You pump more energy into that verse in order to get done what you planned. Doesn't matter that it worked in rehearsal. What matters is what's going on *right now,* onstage, in front of the audience. Playing music, if you want to see it this way, is a real privilege. Stay right in the moment and make the most of it.

#57—LEAVE YOUR EGO
IN THE PARKING LOT

WHY IT MAKES YOU
MORE USEFUL:

You're useful when you play what's needed, but you won't even see it if you think it's all about you. Don't think like an artist—think like a servant.

WHAT TO DO:

Don't be more important than the song. Sometimes the song doesn't need very much from you. If someone needs to shine to make this song happen, get out of the way and let them shine. It's about the ensemble. It's about the result. Don't wait for the leader to tell you this—just back off and let the song be what it needs to be.

THOUGHTS:

If you come to a performance thinking that the audience

owes you their respect, or to let you play something *you* really want to play, you're thinking like a rock star. I don't even know you, and I know you're not a rock star. I don't know any rock stars, and the really good musicians I *do* know care mostly about making the song good and pleasing the audience.

For a season I was the band leader on a local cable access no-budget TV show. I had a little band of guys who played with me, all seasoned and talented players. We'd accompany who-ever our musical guest was, and we taped four shows on Satur-day, once a month. (One of my favorite sayings came from this experience. After an hour or so of setting lights, sound, etc., one of the engineers walked out onto the set and said, "Well, we've run out of reasons not to start...")

Anyway, one week we *were* ready to start the first taping, but our guest singer wasn't there. I called him and his *mom* an-swered the phone. She said, "He's sleeping."

I said, "Well, he's scheduled to sing on our TV show, we're ready to start, and he knew what time to be here. Please wake him up and get him on the road."

She said, "Oh, I hate to wake him up..."

I sort of demanded to speak to him, and she brought him to the phone. When I read him the riot act, he gave me attitude: "Hey, I'll BE there when I CAN, okay? I had a late night."

When he arrived, eventually, I told him my band was ready to play his songs with him, and he said, "Well, no offense, but I have my own background tracks. They're professionally recorded, and I really don't think you guys will sound anywhere near as good."

He turned out, predictably, to be a very forgettable

singer, and then slouched in the guest chair, wearing sunglasses. Whatta weenie.

Not long after we had a woman with us who had sung on Broadway and recorded with a big name record company. Let me tell you—she made US sound good. She just rolled with everything. Whatta pro.

◆ ◆ ◆

#58—SELL THE SONG

WHY IT MAKES YOU MORE USEFUL:

Recognizing that the song won't fly unless you *make* it fly sets you up to work harder.

WHAT TO DO:

Think of the song as a product you're pitching. Make a plan to convince the listener that this song is worth listening to. Is this a sad song? Play it so people cry. Is this a joyous song? Pump it up. Think about the flow of the song and set it up so the emotion is played up as big as you can play it. Ham it up a little.

A simple example:

The verse is about how needy someone was, until they met the love of their life. The chorus is all about how great it is that they're in love. Play the verse softly, then as you come into the chorus, exaggerate the build up. Explode into that chorus, pulling people into the feeling that this love will last a lifetime. *Convince them.*

THOUGHTS:

There's an old showbiz saying: "Authenticity is what sells, so if you can fake that, you've got it made."

Doing this used to feel fake to me. Not any more. When an audience doesn't feel anything, they go home. I hate it when they go home. The lyrics and chords and guitar parts aren't enough—you have to press the emotion of the thing. Make it your job to bring that emotion to life. Look—it's your JOB to do this onstage. Doesn't matter whether it's dance music at a club or worship music at a church. Bring the song to life or get off stage. If I hear about you sleepwalking through a performance, I'll find you and SUCH a lecture you'll get.

#59—FIND OUT WHAT THE AUDIENCE WANTS

WHY IT MAKES YOU MORE USEFUL:

It makes you a good business person.

WHAT TO DO:

This doesn't have to be complicated—just put yourself in their shoes. Did they drive to the park, set up their lawn chairs, unpack the cooler? They're expecting something fun, low-key, entertaining. Is it a bunch of older people? Turn it down. Is it a bar full of millennials drinking $8 beers? Maybe invest in a knit hat. Are you in a rowdy bar full of people that work hard for a living? Keep the hits coming and make sure it's loud. Remember—THEY'RE PAYING YOU.

THOUGHTS:

I made this mistake over and over and over, for a long

time. Here's the inescapable conclusion:

NOBODY cares what you like, what you want, what your performing dream is. Nobody.

They only care about what *they* want, and *that's* what you have to figure out. One time I asked all my Facebook friends in a post, "what song would YOU like hear at a bar?" I was surprised by the answers—which told me I was still out of touch with the audience. Once in a while, if you earn the trust of an audience, you can try to take them someplace they hadn't considered going. But only maybe once in a night, and only after you've played about 30 of their favorite songs. If you play in a church band, lead them in songs they already know for weeks and weeks before you try something new. Again—put yourself in their shoes. THINK like them.

#60—SET YOUR INSTRUMENT LOUD AND THEN CONTROL IT

WHY IT MAKES YOU MORE USEFUL:

This gives you all kinds of headroom, allowing you to play much louder and softer without changing settings.

WHAT TO DO:

When you set your amp or microphone loud, and then play or sing loud the whole time, the sound person will turn you down. When that happens, all you have left is loud. When all you have left is loud, you lose the ability to coax nuances out of your instrument or voice, and that, my friends, is a *tedious* thing to listen to. It's tedious for *you*. Accustom yourself to playing your instrument softly with the volume turned up. It takes a little finesse, but if you can master it, then playing loudly when it's needed is just a matter of hitting it harder without reaching for the volume knob.

Set it a little loud, then talk to the sound person. I'll often say, "If you'll turn me up a little, I PROMISE I'll be a grownup and not play loud the whole time. If you hear me doing that, then turn me down."

Then HOLD BACK. Play most of what you do somewhere in the middle of your volume range, and deal out the loud stuff very, very sparingly.

Here's what happens otherwise: you play loudly at soundcheck, and you get turned down in the monitors and the house. When the music starts, you can't hear yourself very well and you end up blasting your way through everything, throwing nuance and subtlety out the window. The band gets tired of it, you sound like an egotist and nobody wins.

THOUGHTS:

Over and over I've watched this, all my life. And yes— I've BEEN that guy way too many times. I lost my temper once with a guitar player who was playing incredibly loud—so loud that none of us onstage could hear anything but him. And this was OUTDOORS. I turned my keyboard amp up extremely loud and pointed it right at him until he was trying to play the guitar with one hand over his ear. I didn't talk to him for a year, and I live in a small town. As I write this, I'm wondering if or when I was the one playing too loud. If you're reading this, and I was that obnoxiously loud guy...I'm sorry. There's no excuse.

#61—USE THE COUNT-IN TO SET THE FEEL IN EVERYONE'S BONES

WHY IT MAKES YOU MORE USEFUL:

It gets everyone up and running on the feel of a song almost instantly.

WHAT TO DO:

Throw yourself into the count in, and say it with emotion and feeling.

So instead of:

One, two, three, four…(in a bored voice)

Do this:

ONE and-a *TWO* and a chicka-chicka *THREE FOUR*

You get the picture. Two examples come to mind.

The first is Paul McCartney with the Beatles, counting in "I Saw Her Standing There". Before the music even starts, you KNOW this song is going to drive hard. That kind of count-in pulls the band up and into the song.

The second is pretty obscure, but you can find it on Youtube. It's the song, "Happy 'Cause I'm Goin' Home", by Chicago. I giggle with delight every time I hear it, listening to how that rhythm is in the guitar player's bones before he ever plays a note. And that rhythm is in YOUR bones as well, because he makes you *feel* it.

Yeah, you can't grunt out a bunch of syllables onstage, but you could do something like it. And if the audience can't hear, then grunt away. Just do whatever you have to do to get the musicians hearing and feeling.

THOUGHTS:

I used to try to hide the count from the audience. I thought I was supposed to, like it was bad form or something to let them hear or see the count. Then I saw the band at Saddleback Church in California, and that dude just clapped his hands or snapped his fingers or whatever, and counted right out loud in front of God and everybody. I thought, "You can DO THAT?" Well, he did. And when I got back to the church band I was leading, I started doing the same thing. It worked great, and I never looked back.

#62—THINK LIKE AN ARRANGER

WHY IT MAKES YOU MORE USEFUL:

It puts you in the correct mindset, that of being a smaller part of a bigger whole. You'll play better parts and make a better contribution to any ensemble.

WHAT TO DO:

Ask yourself, "How should this song be put together?" Yes, you can ask that, and you *should* ask that. Find a part you can play that complements what the other people are playing and singing, that supports the song, that moves the song farther down the road. Maybe you're playing guitar, and all the song really needs is a little clipped chord on every 2nd and 4th beat. Yeah, you could play a whole bunch of other stuff, but that would be serving yourself and not the song. Play those little hits and be happy that you're making the song groove so good.

Listen to what the others are doing and ask yourself what's missing. Does the groove need accentuating somewhere? Is there a hole in the sonic spectrum that you could fill? What's lacking? Find that thing and fill the gap. Or maybe what the song needs is for you to play almost nothing, or lay out for the first half. A needy player will play something, *anything*, rather than sit out. A confident player plays only what's needed and nothing more.

Always, always, always listen as if you were in the audience. Remember—they care nothing about your ability. They just want to like the music.

Serve the song first, the audience second and yourself last.

THOUGHTS:

Alfred Hitchcock talked about the 'MacGuffin' in filmmaking. It's the thing that everyone in the movie wants, or is trying to get, or the problem everyone is trying to solve. Lose sight of that and your storytelling will wander. When you play in an ensemble, the most important thing is the song. Not your part, not thinking up something cool to play, not getting a chance to show 'what you can really do', but serving the song. The audience doesn't know anything about music theory. Most of them don't even know which instrument is making which sound. Seriously.

There's a wonderful youtube clip from the movie 'Standing In The Shadows of Motown', and you watch a little reunion of some of their star players recreating that Motown sound. It's 'Ain't Too Proud To Beg by the Funk Brothers', if you want to look it up. They put those parts together masterfully! What they end up with is *one sound.* Not the sound of five or six people playing, but *one sound*—a sound that each contributes to. It's magic. Watching that clip, and that movie, is a wonderful education in how to put music together.

Electric guitar players: Not every song needs a solo. And stop, just STOP filling up every measure with everything you can play. Try playing JUST on the 2 & 4, and absolutely nowhere else, and see what that does for the song

Keyboardists: Play less notes. Keep your left hand out of it, or just play little ghost notes with your left hand thumb. Don't put a brick on the sustain pedal and fill up everything from two octaves below middle C to two octaves above. Less is more.

Bassists: I'm begging you—play the bass part. If you play way up high on the first string, the band still needs a bass player. Hit the downbeat and everything else is adornment.

Drummers: 90% of what you play—no, make the 98% —should just be simple and solid. If you play with me and you play nothing clever or complex whatsoever, I'm totally fine with that. Make the song groove, make it move, and I'll have a hard time not kissing you on the lips.

Acoustic guitar players: If you want to interject a 16th note feel into a song, you don't need to play straight 16th's all the time. Just a few of them here and there among mostly 8th note strumming will give the song the feel of 16th's without all the busyness.

CHAPTER 4-LEADING A BAND

I've done a bunch of this. I was the Director of Instrumental Music for a big community church for over 11 years. We did standard praise band stuff, secular rock and roll, and I led the bands for four big, all original seasonal productions—the biggest one selling nearly 10,000 tickets at a public venue. Also, I led my own cover band for about eight years.

In almost every case I was leading a group of amateur, weekend musicians. Some of them were pretty good players, most of them were not. At the church job, I had a big learning curve—they expected new songs all the time, every week, high quality. I had a family to feed so I got good at band-leading pretty fast. It was that or find something else to do. Leading a band is, well...hard. It's work. And there's never, ever, ever enough time. Ever. I hope this helps!

#63—SIMPLIFY
THE CHORDS

WHY IT MAKES YOU
MORE USEFUL:

The musicians you're leading won't waste time wondering what those chord symbols mean, and you'll get up and running on a song more quickly. Along with this, your band will sound smoother and more professional.

WHAT TO DO:

So much of written music is filled with chords that don't need to be there, or just really shouldn't be played. This is especially true of written music for amateur musicians trying to get ready in one rehearsal. Get your sharpie and black out everything you don't need. There are several reasons to do this, but I'll hit the high spots here, and I hope it helps.

1)   Slash chords. If you're playing any instrument other than bass, you really only need to read the chord on the *left* side of the slash. That's the actual chord. The note on the right side of the slash is an alternate bass note. If there's a

bass player, then you don't need to work out how to get that alternate bass note under the bottom of the chord *you're* playing —the bass player already has that covered.

Remember—the audience is hearing your ensemble as a *whole.* They hear all of it together, and if the bass player is covering that note, that's all that counts. Cross out that alternate bass notes on the music you pass out and it will make everything so much easier on the eyes. If you're the bass player, cross out the whatever's on the *left* side of the slash. That's not you.

Yes, I know—that slash chord describes the whole of the harmony at that moment in the music. But in almost every case, but if you're playing piano or guitar, you don't need to try and make it all sound on your instrument. In fact, you probably *shouldn't* try to do that—leaving things out makes a simpler, more listenable sound.

2)   Passing chords. These are chords that fall on the last beat of the measure, and go by very, very quickly. You can almost always do without them. Cross them out.

3)   Keep the chords that fall on the downbeat, and on beat 3—those are almost always important. Question chords that fall on the 2nd and 4th beats.

4)   Chords with big extensions. These are chords like 'F13' or 'G11' or 'E9'. When you see these, change them to simpler '7' chords. Seriously. You won't hurt anything. Think of 9's, 11's ad 13's as neckties for smaller chords. So change that 'F13b9' into an F7 and be happy. Any number bigger than a '7' can be changed to a '7'. So if you see a C9, C11 or C13, change it to a C7. Keep the minor or major, but that's it. Like this: C13, C11, C9 = C7 Cmi13, Cmi11, Cmi9 = Cmi7 Cma13, Cma11, Cma9 = Cma7 Yeah, I know those bigger chords are cool,

and if your band can quickly get to them, then by all means, knock yourself out. But stumbling all over the place because someone doesn't know, or can't get their hands on a complex chord—it's a waste of time.

The written music sometimes just looks so *cluttered.* I see this in charts I've downloaded from SongSelect, the Christian music service that allows you to download charts for worship songs. They get so...*correct* about these things that their charts are sometimes unreadable. They're trying to make sure every single little change in the harmony is reflected in the chords, but in doing so they present something nearly unplayable, and most likely unlistenable.

Play through the chart, listen for the chords you think are the most important and then cross out everything else (at least in pencil until after rehearsal and you're sure what works).

THOUGHTS:

This, in my opinion, is *the single biggest time vampire at rehearsal.* When I worked as a church music director, I *always* took the time to alter those chords before they ever got into the hands of my volunteer musicians. Most of the time they never knew, our rehearsals went far smoother, and we sounded a LOT better because I did this. Conversely, I've been to rehearsals I was not leading, where we spent precious minutes trying to figure out what was wrong, what didn't sound good, fixing and correcting because the chord charts weren't, for lack of a better term, *clean.* Yeah, you'll have to think pretty hard at first, but you'll improve, and it's WORTH IT.

#64—TELL THE STORY

WHY IT MAKES YOU
MORE USEFUL:

When you understand that a song needs to be presented dramatically, your music will have a much stronger effect on listeners.

WHAT TO DO:

Think of a song like a story. Everyone likes a good story.

Good stories have:
Conflict and resolution
A beginning, middle and end
An arc—they start in one place and end in another. One event leads to another and there are plenty of surprises along the way
Interesting characters
A satisfying ending

Making a song listenable—arranging it—is pretty much the same as writing a good story.

Good arrangements, then, have:

An Introduction:

Introduce your song in such a way that it sets things in motion and hints at things to come. If a mostly loud, fast song has a soft part in the middle, use it in the intro. Create a sense of expectation.

Interesting characters (instruments).

Introducing the instruments all at once gives the song lots of energy.

Bringing the instruments in one at a time gives more attention to each one. The unexpected introduction of an instrument can have a powerful effect—use it to draw attention to a particular lyric. Just as in a story, don't introduce an interesting character at the beginning and then never bring it back. Bring an interesting instrument in during the middle and it adds flavor. Bring it in at the end and it will confuse things.

Ebb and flow.

Instruments entering and dropping out, volume changes, tempo changes, etc., keep the song from becoming tedious.

Surprises.

Surprises create interest and keep the audiences attention. A sudden change in volume, tempo, etc., will bring attention to a particular lyric.

Tension.

Playing very loudly, then very quietly, leaving notes hanging, etc., creates a sense of mystery.

A good ending.

The loose ends are tied up, the song has a sense of resolution.

THOUGHTS:

You're telling a story. Is this an exciting song? Start it out big, all of the instruments in at once. Is it a somber song? Start it out slowly, sneaking the instruments in one at a time. Try to match what's happening musically to what's happening lyrically.

If you think about this while you're putting songs together, or just playing your part, you'll start to see the possibilities. Even if you're the only one onstage thinking this way, you can have an effect. If everyone is playing all the time, all the way through, at the very least *you* can drop in and out. It will help. If the song needs to lose energy at some point and nobody realizes it, start playing long, long tones on your instrument. Not only will this help the song breathe and tell its story, but you'll probably find the other musicians responding in kind.

It's kind of a little miracle when you make music. You create vibrations in the air, and somewhere between you and the eardrum of the listener, it's turned into *emotion.* That's really quite a cool, mysterious, thing. If you think about a song this way, you'll understand your job better—to move the audience by the short little story of a song.

#65—PLAY TO YOUR MUSICIANS' STRENGTHS

WHY IT MAKES YOU MORE USEFUL:

The band will sound much better, and your players will feel more confident and relaxed.

WHAT TO DO:

Whatever a musician is good at, see if you can find a way to use it. Some drummers have a beat they really love, some guitarists are at good at the blues, your piano player may know a lot of chords. It goes like this with everyone. Rather than force them into a role they can't fill, figure out what role they're already equipped to fill, and then put them there. Even if you change the song a little more than you'd like to, it's still worth it.

The better you understand your players and the better you understand music, the more you can make this approach work for you.

THOUGHTS:

There was a guitar player in my church band who was totally rock and roll. If we could play Led Zeppelin and Tom Petty songs all morning (we couldn't), it would fit him exactly right. So when I knew he'd be on for a particular weekend, I'd start already in the service planning meetings (weeks ahead), steering the song selection toward things I knew he'd be strong in. Then when I picked prelude and offering songs, I'd pick songs with a rock feel. This was not only for his benefit, but for ours--when he was in his element, the music was much more powerful.

If the song warranted it, I'd give him a solo. He had a great sound. Then I'd give him a little guidance. The blues scale and all things blues were his domain. But if you move your hand down three frets on the guitar neck you get a much 'sweeter' sound, a more major feel, and all the notes work. So we'd be in the key of A, but the song didn't have a hard edge to it, so I'd make a note on his music: Solo F# Blues. This allowed him to play all his great licks and still fit the song. (He could have got there on his own, but he owned his own business, and making that note for him in the music saved him probably 15 minutes of listening and working things out.)

In my own band I had a guitar player who was very, very strong with lead guitar stuff, but not as solid on the rhythm stuff. So I would usually hold down the middle of the sound, playing more rhythmic, chordal stuff on either piano or guitar. That left him open to play tasty licks in all the empty spots, which he was good at, and he'd often solo in the middle of a song. The audience won because they loved to watch him take solos—he could be spectacular. He won because he loved to do this. And I won because my band sounded the best it could.

#66—GET RID OF TRICKY RHYTHMIC PASSAGES

WHY IT MAKES YOU MORE USEFUL:

The musicians you're leading will be up and running and feeling the music far, far more quickly.

WHAT TO DO:

Everybody automatically thinks and hears and feels the music in sets of 2, 4, 8 and 16 bars. Same number of beats in every bar, no surprises. That's a strong position from which to approach every song. Read through the music and look for spots where someone got, well, *fancy* with the arrangement. Does the chorus end with a weird little bar tacked on? Either get rid of it or make it two bars. Is there one lonely measure of 3/4 or 2/4 time in an otherwise smoothly flowing line of 4/4? Make it a 4/4 bar. Your goal is to flow effortlessly, logically all the way through.

THOUGHTS:

I do this all the time when I'm in charge of a band, and half the time or more, no one even notices. I'm serious. If you have a drummer who *does* notice and wants to do the tricky part, and a bass player who stumbles over that same part every time, then your rehearsal time is better spent convincing the quick-thinking drummer to just play it straight than to try and rehearse the bass player into playing the tricky part. Chances are very great that the bass player will flub it onstage no matter how hard he works.

This is especially true in situations where you have only a little rehearsal time—which is pretty much always. However, even in bands with really, really good musicians, this is not a bad idea.

In my dance band we played 'You Keep Me Hanging On', by the Supremes. Killer song, and we played a great version of it. But it had one verse, maybe the third verse, where there were two measures different than all the other times. I could never keep it straight. I'm pretty good at all this, but I stumbled over it every single time. I was distracted, I was leading the band, I was making decisions on the fly, thinking of other things that needed attending, I didn't feel like memorizing it. Whatever—I stumbled over it. So the guitar player would keep track of this. He'd catch my eye and hold up two fingers, or grin and lean into the passage. However he did it, he always signaled me that THIS was the time we dropped two bars.

That wasn't a bad solution, but I'm here to tell you—if we'd made that passage like the others in the song, *nobody would have known.* Literally. The dancers would not have stopped dancing and looked up to say, "Hey, aren't there two less bars there?" The Supremes aficionados in the audience might have thought "...was that right?" I lobbied to change it, but my bandmates held fast—we were playing it *wrong* if we didn't drop the two bars.

Do you see my point? Little things like that matter to musicians, but not to anyone else. So keep the big picture in mind.

#67—DIVIDE RHYTHMS AND RANGES

WHY IT MAKES YOU MORE USEFUL:

The parts will fit better together and be easier to mix.

WHAT TO DO:

If you can, move your players into various non-conflicting parts. (Players can be SO sensitive about being 'told' what to play, so walk softly) Listen to what everyone is playing, and help them pick a rhythm and range that doesn't conflict with someone else. Think in terms of quarter notes, eighths and sixteenths for the rhythms, and one octave ranges for the notes.

Is the piano playing chords down around middle C? Move the acoustic guitar up the neck with a capo to get out of the way. Is the drummer playing a very busy part? Keep everyone else a little simpler. If the guitar is strumming a sixteenth feel, you need longer chords on the piano. If the piano player is playing arpeggios, keep the guitars to longer, more fluid strumming.

The more work you do in advance of rehearsal, the easier this will be—preparing capo charts, making notes on the music sheets, etc. Be careful you don't put someone in an awkward position.

This is not a hard and fast rule, but it *will* have a positive effect if you keep it in mind. It will definitely solve sound problems.

THOUGHTS:

Leon Russell, the famous Wrecking Crew piano player, said he became known for playing parts higher up the keyboard —but the only reason he did it was because he wanted to be *heard* on the recording, and if he played in the middle of the piano, he'd be buried in the mix. Being heard meant getting noticed, and getting noticed meant getting more work.

This is actually a function of thinking like an arranger **(see #62--Think Like An Arranger)**. When everyone is in exactly the same note range, and plays the same basic rhythms, that's a recipe for a muddy, undefined sound. The end product you want is for the entire band to sound like one well-articulated instrument.

When someone takes an instrumental solo, help the other players see that they need to watch and listen, working constantly to stay out of the soloist's way. If the soloist moves up, they move down, and vice versa. If the soloist is playing a busy part, playing lots of notes, the rest of the band needs to play less. This takes practice because everyone's instinct will be to jump in on the soloist's energy and follow right along—keep an eye on this! Cultivate the practice of doing the opposite.

◆ ◆ ◆

#68—BUILD THE SONG FROM THE BOTTOM UP

WHY IT MAKES YOU MORE USEFUL:

When you understand the foundation, you can help the band to make it strong.

WHAT TO DO:

If the bottom end of an arrangement isn't right, you can't fix it by changing the top end. This applies specifically to ensembles with drums and bass. If the drums and bass are solid together, the other instruments can get away with murder and the song will still feel good. Time and energy spent on this *always* pays off.

If there's no drummer, the bass player plays a much greater roll. Help the bassist to play solidly, telegraphing the basic direction of every part of the song. Also, a very simple and solid piano or guitar part could help make up for having no drummer. Make the bottom end solid *first,* then move on to the other instruments. A solid foundation also makes it much easier for the other instruments to hear what needs to be played, to find their place.

THOUGHTS:

It's all about the foundation, pretty much exactly like building a house. The bass line plays a strong role in defining the harmony for the listener, because it's usually sitting on the fundamental tone of whatever chord is going by. (By fundamental, I mean the note that names the chord. The fundamental of a Cma7 chord is a C).

Whatever instrument you play, even if you're not the leader, see if you can help the bassist and drummer do this well. Sometimes I just listen for something the bass or drummer is doing that really works, and I verbally compliment them on it.

"Oh man, I loved that little thing you guys did on the chorus, locking up the kick drum and bass. So cool."

Or,

"On that third verse, I think it'd be great if you played that really simple, solid thing you did on the intro."

Also, when I hear the bottom end working great, I'll often turn to the bassist and drummer and sort of visibly get into the groove with them. Musicians *love* it when someone notices something they do, and complimenting them on it means you'll probably get more of it.

#69—MAKE THE INTRO
A REPEATING LOOP

WHY IT MAKES YOU
MORE USEFUL:

This greatly reduces the possibility of getting off to a bad start.

WHAT TO DO:

Make the intro a four bar loop, something that could repeat over and over. If you need your intro to be longer, then start with fewer instruments and add someone every time the first bar comes back around. What this does is pretty nearly completely eliminate the train wreck of a singer coming in wrong. Use chords that make it easy to sense the first verse coming. That might even be the four bars that end the chorus, which will give the singer the feeling that the verse is coming.

So if your song starts on a C chord in the key of C, do this:

F - - - | - - - - |G - - - |G7 - - - | (acoustic guitar only)
F - - - | - - - - |G - - - |G7 - - - | (add bass)

F - - - | - - - - |G - - - |G7 - - - | (add drums)

By the time you get to the C chord, everyone will be ready to hear it.

THOUGHTS:

The beauty of this is that everyone relaxes. This works REALLY good when you have to get several songs ready in a hurry, or you're doing new songs all the time (like you do in a church band). There are a million things that could mess with the beginning of a song: the pastor decides to pray on a whim, a door slams really loud backstage, someone's amp makes a noise, the singer walks onstage late, the singer decides to talk before the he starts, fire trucks go by outside—you get the picture.

If your intro can only be played one way, and you flub it, your only choice at that point is to start over. That's awkward every time. This way you can keep playing, drop instruments in and out, and STILL get the song up and running right.

When I lead the band at my little church, I intro every song, every time, doing this. The rest of the players join in when they feel it.

(See #70—USE THE INTRO TO SET UP THE FEEL)

#70—USE THE INTRO
TO SET UP THE FEEL

WHY IT MAKES YOU
MORE USEFUL:

Good intros set the feel of the song in everyone's head and hands.

WHAT TO DO:

Don't be clever with the intro. That's WAY overrated. Instead, use the intro to get the feeling of the song into both the band and the listener's heads and hands. This is more important that anything else you can do in an intro. The intro HAS to get everyone up and running, feeling the rhythm and pulse of the song. I've talked elsewhere about the count-in, which is also part of the intro. But there's more to it. When the intro is done, everyone in the room should have a strong, solid feeling for how this song is going to go.

THOUGHTS:

A 6/8 feel is, for instance, hard to get going until everyone feels it. Get it wrong, and you're in trouble. And some inexperienced musicians have trouble with that feel. So pick your strongest player onstage to play four bars of that 6/8 groove on their instrument. Maybe it's the acoustic guitar, maybe it's the bass, maybe it's the drums. Doesn't matter. Let that person settle everyone in, and THEN start adding instruments. Maybe the acoustic player just scratches on deadened strings, maybe that's all you need. While they're doing that, sing the chorus of the song in your head so you're matching up to it.

DON'T play the original recorded intro to a song if you can't get the feel right. And listen—very often on these recordings, the band is playing one or two isolated instruments along with a rhythm track *you can't hear.* They're listening to it on headphones in the recording studio, playing or singing along with it. That way they get the feel just right. It's a neat trick, but you can't do that onstage. Instead, do whatever you have to do to get the feeling right. Do that and you've launched yourself properly.

(See #69—*MAKE THE INTRO A REPEATING LOOP*)

#71—LAY YOUR CHARTS OUT LOGICALLY

WHY IT MAKES YOU MORE USEFUL:

It makes the charts more readable. This saves time, and everybody relaxes as they play through it.

WHAT TO DO:

However you do your music—words & chords, actual staves, or chords laid out with slashes—set everything up in sets of four or 8 bars. So instead of this:

```
C---|----|Ami---|----|F---|----|G---|----|C---|F---|
G---|----|Ami---|F---|G---|----|C---|----|Ami---|----|F--
-|----|G---|----|C---|F---|G---|----|Ami---|F---|G---|----|
```

Or worse, *this:*

C Ami F G C F G

```
Ami F G C Ami F G C F
G Ami F G
```

Lay it out this way:

```
C  - - -  |- - - -|Ami - - -|- - - -|
F  - - -  |- - - -|G - - -  |- - - -|
C  - - -  |F- - - G  - - -  |- - - -|
Ami - - -|F- - -|G - - -  |- - - -| (REPEAT)
```

Do you see I even played around with the dashes and lines to make everything line up? That's a far, far easier chart to read. Also, leave space enough between the sections that you can easily tell which one is which.

If you're doing a words/chords chart, lay everything out the way the words logically fit—line by line. Try to keep the same number of lines in every section. It also helps, if you're doing just chords on a page, to write the first few lyrics of each section right above that section, in quotes. That way the musicians can follow the singer, should they skip around.

THOUGHTS:

Your players will automatically, almost instantly see how the song goes, and they'll be able to find their place in the song immediately should they get lost or should there be an on-stage call to repeat a section. Also, this kind of chart is easy to make notes on with a pencil. You can often get the whole song on one sheet of paper with room enough to not look cluttered.

#72—DIRECT INSTEAD OF MEMORIZING

WHY IT MAKES YOU MORE USEFUL:

It saves a TON of time, and relieves the stress of wondering if everyone is remembering everything.

WHAT TO DO:

This is useful if you're leading a band in a situation where you're doing different songs every week and rotating players (like in a praise band at a church). Instead of working them at rehearsal until they've memorized every little thing, (or you HOPE they've memorized every little thing...it's a lot to ask), set up some simple hand signals and have them just keep their eyes on you.

Fist in the air = it's the last time through
Finger twirling in the air = go around again, or keep going
Open hand pushing downward = pull back, drop down

Just make sure YOU know where the changes are!

THOUGHTS:

Again this is something I learned watching the band at Saddleback Church. The leader also taught us this in a smaller session. When I got back to my church, I started doing this, with a BIG emphasis on getting the drummer to watch me. In fact I pushed the grand piano off the stage and started playing keyboards so I could set up right in the middle of the band. If we were bringing it way down for the third verse, I would look over at him until he felt my eyes on him, and then I'd give him the open-hand-pushing-downward sign. When he saw that, he'd think, "Oh yeah, we're bringing it down for this verse."

Not only did we do a much better job of playing dynamically onstage, but we cut back on rehearsal time as well. Another benefit was that the band relaxed about 1,000 percent—they no longer feared they'd miss a cue. This kept it fun for my volunteers, and warded off burnout.

Once in a while I'D miss the cue, but that's another story...

#73—MAKE ROOM FOR OTHER MUSICIAN'S CREATIVITY

WHY IT MAKES YOU MORE USEFUL:

You'll foster a sense of community.

WHAT TO DO:

Give your fellow musicians room to express themselves. Resist the urge to dictate—use that as a last resort. Yeah, you may have a specific end in mind, but see first if you can get there by letting the musicians come up with their own thing. Be open to someone interpreting something in a way you would not have. Is there a particular guitar solo on a recording that your band is covering? See what the guitar player thinks, and be open to something else. Is the drummer playing a beat that's not quite the same as the recording, or not what you'd hoped for? Let it go for a while and see what develops.

Musicians get into this all to express themselves. It's a

HUGE part of their motivation. Maybe sometimes their ONLY motivation. Yeah, it'd be nice to fire them and get someone who'll do a better job, but this isn't the LA Studio Scene. You don't live in that world. You live in a world of local musicians who long to feel included, to express themselves, and who have likely spent a LOT of time imagining what it'll be like when they finally, finally get to express themselves onstage. Give everyone room to breathe. Yes, you have a job to do onstage, but if you can get it done *and* accommodate the self-expression of your bandmates, you're making for a great experience.

THOUGHTS:

I saw this at a big church conference in Chicago. Everything onstage just *oozed* perfection. The curtain rose, the drummer counted in to a metronome (I could see the metronome in his drum cage and I could see him pushing buttons), the lights came on, and the song started perfectly. Too perfectly. It was great, but it was...stiff. I could just *feel* the musicians thinking 'I can't mess this up, I can't mess this up'. The players looked like they'd come straight from a morning meeting at IBM, but there was one guy that looked out of place to me--long hair, jeans, etc. I assumed they just couldn't get anybody else, and I think I remember some beads or something hanging down from the headstock of his guitar. They gave him an 8 bar solo in the middle of the opening song, and it was wooden and over-rehearsed. It sounded like he'd been *forced* to play these particular notes. I felt for him. Maybe there were extenuating circumstances, but I found myself thinking, *'Come on—couldn't you just let him take those 8 bars wherever he wanted? What could it have hurt?'*

Don't do that to musicians. Let them have a little fun.

◆ ◆ ◆

CHAPTER 5-GENERAL MUSICIANSHIP

I've wanted to be a good musician all my life, starting the night I saw The Beatles on Ed Sullivan. It seemed then, as now, like the coolest, most important thing a person could ever hope to be. For probably 20 years, starting when I was about 14, I thought about it constantly, begged or boasted my way into playing situations, and annoyed every good musician I ran into by asking endless questions. I would listen to a record, try to imitate what I heard, lifting up the needle and setting it back to the beginning of the song over and over. Cassettes, and later CD's saved me a lot of work, being easier to rewind. All these years later...not a lot has changed. It still calls to me, still seems like if I can just make those magic sounds, I'll be in on the biggest secret ever. It's a fascinating, never-ending endeavor.

◆ ◆ ◆

#74—LEARN ABOUT
OTHER INSTRUMENTS

WHY IT MAKES YOU
MORE USEFUL:

It makes you a better ensemble player. The better you understand what the instruments onstage are doing (and how they do it), the better you'll fit in.

WHAT TO DO:

Listen and analyze. Spend time listening to recordings and see if you can pick out what everybody's doing. Start with drums. Can you picture a drum kit with its various pieces? If you can't, then watch a video to get the lay of the land. Once you're familiar with a drum kit, listen and think. Is he hitting the hi hats on 8th notes? The kick drum, the snare? On which beats is he hitting them all? Is there one combination for the verse, another for the chorus? Try to get inside his head. Ask yourself why he made those choices. Do the same thing with the bass. Often the bass player will lock in with the kick drum to build a solid foundation for the groove—is that what's happening here? And so on.

Do this with every instrument you don't play, and don't be afraid to ask musicians what they're thinking when they play. (You'll get mixed results with this. Some musicians can't easily articulate what they're playing. Be patient, draw them out.)

THOUGHTS:

My friend Joe pulled me up short one day. I bragged to him that I could sing the entire lead line along with a Maynard Ferguson big band recording. It was fairly complex and a long song, so I was proud. He said, "Yeah, but can you sing the trombone part, Eddie? You gotta know what everybody else is doing, too."

I had to think about that. Why would that matter? What do I care what the trombones are playing? What possible difference could that make? But he was right. I listened to the trombones, and whaddya know?—I heard things I'd completely missed. I understood the song better. If you can sing or mimic or at least understand the other parts being played, you can jump in with a rhythm they're playing, or play their part in unison for part of a passage. This is *great* stuff.

Duane Allman, the celebrated guitarist, said that he spent a whole year only listening to Miles Davis' influential album, 'Kind Of Blue'. Said he just couldn't listen to anything else.

Wait, what? What does moody trumpet jazz have to do with country rock? I don't know what Allman heard, but he heard *something*. Something that influenced his guitar playing. I'm not terribly familiar with Allman's recordings, but I'm pretty sure if I listened to 'Kind Of Blue' for a year, I'd hear it in his playing.

One more, since you've read this far. Artie Shaw, the influential clarinetist, band leader, arranger and composer in the 30's and 40's was asked about Benny Goodman, his closest rival: "When I first met Benny Goodman, he wouldn't talk about anything but the clarinets, mouthpieces, reeds, etc. When I tried to change the subject, he said, 'But that's what we have in common. We both play clarinet.' I said, 'No, Benny, that's where we're different. You play clarinet, I play music'". Ouch.

Look past the surface and see what's *really* going on. It's fascinating. It might be a slow process for you. Don't quit. Make yourself useful.

#75—LEARN A NEW
SONG EVERY WEEK

WHY IT MAKES YOU
MORE USEFUL:

It sharpens your ability to learn and digest new things quickly. It improves your ear. It stores yet another concrete, real-world example of music in your head, something you will surely draw on someday. Someday something will come out of your hands during a song, and you'll think, "Where did THAT come from?". Pretty good chance it came from something you learned a long time ago.

WHAT TO DO:

Pick a good song, a classic song in the genre you like, a song you'll likely be asked to play at some point, and learn everything about it you can. Make a chord chart for it by copying the lyrics from a website and pasting them into your word processor. Then listen and write the chords down over the words. DON'T rely on the chords from the internet or a song book, unless you really get stumped. Listen and learn. Figure out what your instrument is doing on the song, then listen for a while to what everybody else is playing and work out how it all fits together. If you *really* want to be ambitious, try to actually transcribe the song—the actual notes.

When you're done with all this you'll have digested a TON of stuff, and it will swirl around in your head forever. It will come out of your hands at some point. It will make you a better musician. It will work the music into your bones.

THOUGHTS:

I did this every week for eleven years as the director of instrumental music at a big church. They'd say, "Let's do this song!", and there would be no music for it. So I'd sit with the CD player and the keyboard in front of me and start. I was already good at it (because I've been unable to stop myself from doing it since I was 16), but as you might guess, it sharpened my ear considerably to do this all the time.

Sometimes the chords are hard to pick out if there are lots of instruments. Be patient and listen over and over to just the thing you're trying to hear. It will bubble to the top after several listenings.

You don't have to start with the intro or the first verse. In fact, I've found that later verses are often stripped of excess instruments and the basic chords are easier to hear. Also, the intro is probably drawn from some passage in the verse or chorus, and once you're figured those out, it will be easier to pick up.

This, right here, what I've just described, is probably the next best thing to an actual musical education, and in some ways it might be better. (Well, that's my opinion. Listen to your parents...) It forces you to hear and learn things as they are presented in the real world.

◆ ◆ ◆

#76—MAKE SURE YOUR EQUIPMENT WORKS

WHY IT MAKES YOU MORE USEFUL:

It keeps you focused on more important things, and it sends the message that you're competent.

WHAT TO DO:

Keep your stuff in good condition! The goal here is *no surprises.* It's beginner-level to fix anything that's broken, but take it one step farther—check your equipment regularly to make sure no problems are lurking just around the corner. If you're a wind player, get the pads replaced on a regular schedule. If you play keyboard, check all the cables, knobs, etc., regularly. Guitar and bass, change your strings regularly, buy a tube tester and make sure your amp is working. Keep spares. Do all this before trouble shows up onstage, because you'll look, at the very least, dumb. At worst, completely incompetent. Oh—and bring a backup instrument if at all possible.

THOUGHTS:

Sure, things can go wrong. I once had the output jack on my Fender Jaguar come un-soldered onstage. The guitar went dead. At the next break we took it apart and attempted to solder the wires back on with a lighter, but it didn't work. Thankfully the other guitar player had a spare guitar, and I played that the rest of the night.

If I could, I'd bring a backup of every single thing. I don't, for the obvious reasons, but I'd feel better if I did.

Mostly, this kind of trouble is avoidable. Do your best to understand how your instrument and equipment work so you can anticipate trouble. If you're terrible with technical stuff (like I mostly am), then pay someone to do it for you. Just don't get caught looking dumb.

(See #25—STOP BLAMING YOUR EQUIPMENT)

#77—LISTEN TO OLDER MUSIC

WHY IT MAKES YOU MORE USEFUL:

It illuminates the music you're already playing, providing valuable, sometimes priceless insights into how the music goes together.

WHAT TO DO:

Read interviews with the artists you really admire, and find out who *they* were listening to when they were getting started. Then see if you can find out who *those* people were listening to. Run it back as far as you can, and then start from that point and listen forward. For instance:

You hear the Beach Boys' influence in popular music to this day, especially in beautiful soaring harmonies. The mind behind the Beach Boys was Brian Wilson. Wilson grew up listening to, and being obsessed with the harmonies of The Four Freshmen. The Four Freshmen were listening to Mel Torme and The Meltones. So Youtube your way through about 20 minutes of The Meltones, then The Four Freshmen, then the Beach Boys. You'll likely be astonished.

If you REALLY want to do this right, figure out some of these songs and digest them. Make your own handwritten chart, memorize the song, get it into your bones. You'll never, ever regret it.

THOUGHTS:

When I was 14 or 15 years old my grandmother's neighbor traded us her really cool stereo for our old one. We had an old cabinet style turntable. It played everything in mono. Hers was a gadgety unit that folded open. So cool. The turntable folded down and the speakers swung out, and you could even detach them and set them as far apart as the wires allowed. And it was stereo!

Along with it, she gave me a record: 'Jerry Gray Plays Glenn Miller Hits.' I had only a vague idea who Glenn Miller was, but my dad had a big smile on his face. He loved that stuff. I was immediately fascinated by that record. This was, I learned from my dad, the music that young people were listening and dancing to in the 1930's and early 1940's. I sat at the piano trying to figure out the basic chords of Tuxedo Junction, String of Pearls, Moonlight Serenade, etc. In the process, that music got down a little into my bones. Several years later I bought a two-record set of Glenn Miller's band recorded live from the radio. Better equipped to listen, I figured out a bunch more, digesting these songs even better. It turns out that when I later became obsessed with the Beach Boys, guess what I heard? The same harmonies. That same music I listened to filtered down through popular music for decades, informing the music I loved.

Broaden yourself. Listen to jazz, gospel, R&B, pop—from all eras. You want a kick? Find a recording of Junior Walker & The Allstars 'Shotgun' (60's Motown), turn it up LOUD on a good sound system and then ask yourself if you hear mid-80's R&B. Not familiar with mid-80's R&B? Dig a little!

#78—EDUCATE YOURSELF ABOUT SOUND

WHY IT MAKES YOU MORE USEFUL:

Your own instrument will sound better because you'll understand how the sound gets from you to the audience. Also, you'll be able to make suggestions in an informed way.

WHAT TO DO:

Read, listen, ask questions. When you're all set up on-stage, go back to the sound board and just observe. Sound people, if they're not too busy, LOVE to talk about sound. So ask questions when the time is right. If you have extra time, ask if there's something you can do to help. Just understanding the basics of good sound reinforcement will help immensely when you're trying to get a good sound out of your own instrument.

THOUGHTS:

The world of live music is jam-packed with sound people who don't know very much, or who don't know anything, but are nevertheless in charge of making YOU sound good. A little knowledge might be your best friend here.

One Sunday morning at The Big Church, I was not onstage. It was a rare Sunday off the stage for me, so I was up in the sound booth listening. As I listened, I realized I couldn't hear the piano very well, and we had a guest playing it. He was a good player. So I asked the sound guy if we could turn the piano up. He said, "I tried, but it just keeps feeding back." (It was a grand piano with a mic on it).

I asked if I could tinker, and he said, "By all means." As I listened, I realized that the acoustic guitar was playing a lot of open chords, which put him right in the same range as the piano player, who was playing in the middle of the piano. So I rolled a little of the low frequencies out of the acoustic guitar, and some of the midrange as well. This gave us the sound of the acoustic without all the deepness. Then I cut the highs on the piano a little. It was all that was needed. The piano and the guitar now occupied different sonic ranges, and each of them could be heard separately. When I then turned the piano up a little, it popped right out in the mix.

Sneaky advice: don't let on how much you know, unless you need to. It's great to know this stuff, but if you brag about it, or show your hand too much, you'll end up being asked to do a bunch of extra stuff. You can't fix the whole world.

#79—DON'T EVER BE TOO GOOD FOR A SONG

WHY IT MAKES YOU MORE USEFUL:

When you embrace a song, no matter how simple, you set yourself up to play the best possible version of that song for your circumstances.

WHAT TO DO:

Drop the posing and respect the song. Simple songs, *good* simple songs are hard to write, and deserve respect. Don't believe you can improve the song by adding something really clever and complicated—you probably can't. Relax, play simply, play only what's needed, and enjoy the music. Concentrate on making the song *feel* good. If you're not enjoying the song, chances are your audience isn't either.

THOUGHTS:

Complicated doesn't = good, simple doesn't = bad. That's missing the point.

One night at rehearsal I said to my band, "This weekend let's play 'Wild Thing' by The Troggs. There was eye-rolling, and 'come on, man', and 'Jeez, Ed—that song is just so *dumb.*' But I held my ground, and that weekend in front of a crowd I turned to the band and said, "We're doing Wild Thing. I got a feeling about this one."

To the audience, I said, "We're going straight for the gutter." And then I turned my amp up loud and played the opening chords—loud, raucous, utterly devoid of finesse. I hit the guitar strings so hard they rattled on the fretboard. The reaction was electric. Chairs scraped back, people jostled each other to get out on the dance floor and the looks of joy on their faces was, well—it was just so much fun. Playing a complex song onstage, and playing it well is satisfying, no doubt—but it's not NEARLY as much fun as someone leaping to their feet and saying to their neighbor, "Oh, I LOVE this song!!"

#80—LENGTHEN YOUR PHRASES

WHY IT MAKES YOU MORE USEFUL:

It makes your playing much easier to listen to, and it keeps things from getting tedious.

WHAT TO DO:

Don't play the same thing, bar after bar. Don't strum exactly the same way, playing exactly the same beat, whatever, over and over. Turn a one-measure phrase into a four-measure phrase. Find something to play at the end of the second measure that's just a little different. That gives you a two-bar phrase. Then find something yet again different at the end of the fourth bar—making this now a four bar phrase. This gives your playing contour, adding little ups and downs to the feel, and it sits much better in the groove.

For instance:

You're strumming an acoustic in a song with a basic 8th

note feel. You're strumming up and down:

One-and-two-and-three-and-four-and

On the second measure, leave out the first 'and', so you're playing:

One...two-and-three-and-four-and

Third measure same as the first.

Fourth measure, only play one of the 'ands':

One...two, three-and-four.

So, like this:

Chicka, chicka, chicka, chicka
Chick, chicka, chicka, chicka
Chicka, chicka, chicka, chicka
Chick, chick, chicka, chick

You get the idea. *What* you do isn't as important as just doing *something*.

Because you're probably not doing this in a void, listen to the musicians around you and see if there's something you can jump in on. Is there something another musician is doing that you could incorporate? Maybe the bass player has a little thing he or she does every so often—see if you can steal it for your instrument and make a pattern out of it. Every time it comes around for the bassist, you're reinforcing it.

THOUGHTS:

This requires mental effort, because it's really, really easy to just fall into a simple pattern. However, if you're doing this on a song you'll play often, you can count on your four-bar pattern becoming habit. This is especially true if you're singing while you play. Practice at home doing your new, longer phrase while you sing, until it becomes habit.

#81—PLAY INTO THE GROOVE

WHY IT MAKES YOU MORE USEFUL:

Your playing will have a far, far better *feeling* to it.

WHAT TO DO:

Find the notes that are strongly accented in any song (usually the 2 & 4, but not always), and hit them a little stronger than the other notes you play. You don't necessarily have to change the part you're playing, just hit those particular notes harder, or shorter, or whatever you have to do to accent them.

One-and-TWO-and-three-and-FOUR-and

Strum that way, hit those piano notes or chords just a little harder. Learn to get the feeling of this right down into your bones. In 3/4 time it's usually the 3rd beat, so:

One-and-two-and-THREE-and

THOUGHTS:

Playing into the groove is more important than playing the right notes. I'm serious. If your music feels good, the audience will connect with you and forgive all your wrong notes. If your playing is flat, all your correct notes will have been for nothing.

I can't tell you how often I hear players ignoring the groove. It's like a dripping faucet, tedious and annoying. But if you do this right, the people you play with will probably say, "I'm not sure why, but it's just...*better* when that person plays with us." The audience will say, "Man, they sound good, don't they?"

If you're skeptical, try this: Record yourself playing absolutely straight, with no accents, and then play it again the way I'm suggesting. You'll be amazed.

Make this an automatic part of your playing.

#82—LEARN TO LOVE
THE GROOVE

WHY IT MAKES YOU
MORE USEFUL:

Your ability to make a song feel good, to make it swing, to make it drive, to make it work—THAT will get you asked back. THAT will bring the audience to it's feet. THAT will pull up the other players around you and energize them.

WHAT TO DO:

Fall in love with the groove. The groove is how the song feels, simply put. It's the combination of notes and rhythms. Every single time you play a song, ask yourself how it should *feel.* Make this—are you ready?—*the most important thing you address.* Make it your passion. Whenever you listen to a song, *feel along with it.* How the music feels is primary, so make it your first job to get that feel into your bones. Work *first* to make your part feel good, to project an infectious beat, a languid arpeggio, whatever it is—concentrate on that, and *then* work on getting the chords and notes right.

THOUGHTS:

I knew early on, probably by the time I was 16, that I was missing something. I was in a music store in the mall (this was probably 1972), and they had a Clavinet. The Clavinet is the keyboard Stevie Wonder played so well, that funky, plucked sound, kinda like a harpsichord. Anyway, I played a few notes on it, thought I made it sound pretty good. And then this young black guy, maybe 14 years old, walked past and casually played a couple of the funkiest notes I'd ever heard. I thought, 'How did he do that??'.

Several years later I was working with a black singer and I lamented to him that I knew I was missing something, but I didn't know what it was. He said, "Eddie, if you want to play black people's music authentically, you need to learn to love repetition. If you can be happy playing the same thing over and over and over, just for the joy of how it feels, you'll be on your way." I never forgot that, and I determined to make it a priority. I think a LOT of musicians miss this, concentrating instead on being clever or sophisticated.

You wouldn't *believe* what you can get away with when your playing feels good. Here's a field trip for you, if you're up for it. Find an African-American church with a reputation for good music, go there on a Sunday morning and listen closely to what's being played. It's ALL about the feel with this style of music. You'll hear mistakes, and you'll realize you don't care. Some of these players are amazing, but they make it feel good above all else. Some of these players aren't very good at all—but the feel they project makes up for it.

#83—EMPHASIZE ALONG WITH THE SNARE

WHY IT MAKES YOU MORE USEFUL:

You'll be reinforcing the feel of the song, making it much more powerful.

WHAT TO DO:

I've addressed this elsewhere, but here's a refresher: watch the drummer, figure out when he's hitting the snare drum, and whatever you're playing on *that* beat, emphasize it by either hitting it harder or clipping it shorter (or both). This is a little-talked-about skill, but I consider it to be a crucial part of good playing. It should be automatic.

THOUGHTS:

This makes an immediate, noticeable difference. You'll

have to practice it, but you can eventually get to the point where you're emphasizing single notes in the middle of a run, along with the snare. Your listeners and bandmates will probably not be thinking, "Hey, listen to how he's emphasizing along with the snare!" But the listeners will be thinking, "Hey, that sounds good!", and your bandmates will be thinking, "Man, I love it when he plays with us." Everybody wins.

#84—PLAY ON THE BACK OF THE BEAT

WHY IT MAKES YOU MORE USEFUL:

Your playing will feel so, so good. Remember—feel trumps cleverness every time.

WHAT TO DO:

What you're after is to play anything that lands on the 2nd or 4th beats just a tiny bit late. I know it sounds weird, but it's a common practice, and it works really great. Practice this simple thing until you can do it. Listen to old R&B records and see if you can hear it. Listen to newer hip-hop, and you can hear them playing the 2 & 4 so lazy and late that it almost makes it to the next beat. Work on it until you can make it feel lazy like that. Music from Motown and Stax Records are a good place to start, especially the stuff from the mid-late 60's.

THOUGHTS:

My friend and mentor Joe said to me one time, "You're playing on the front of the beat, Eddie. Play on the back." I had no idea what he meant.

He said, "Whatever you're playing when you hit the two and four beats, make it a little *late*." I argued with him, and told him that wasn't possible. You were either *on* the beat, or you *weren't.*

He smiled maddeningly at me and said, "You're wrong. Great players know how to do this. It gives the song a better groove."

I still didn't believe him, but mostly because I couldn't hear it myself. And I was stubborn.

But...one day, driving the Foam Rubber Company delivery truck (yet another of my day jobs), I heard the Beatles "Twist And Shout" on the radio. I'd heard this song *many* times. But to my surprise and delight I heard something I'd missed all those years—I heard Ringo hanging back on the 2nd and 4th beats when he hit the snare. I heard it! I could barely believe it. When I got back to the shipping department I rushed in and played a simple drumbeat on a box of foam, saying to my friend Ralf (a really good drummer), "Look what I just figured out!' He said, "Man, Ed, you really got that feel going there!" I was giddy.

Later I read an interview with Steve Cropper, who played the guitar on a lot of those great Stax Record hits. (He played with the Blues Brothers band in the first movie, I think) He said their studio band worked very hard to get that backbeat feel into their music. But this next part is just so great—when they came out of a big section into a smaller one, they all agreed that (are you ready for this?) on the very first beat #2 in the new section, *they'd move to the center of the beat for one hit only, just on the 2nd beat, to sort of 'push reset' on the feel. Then they'd move right back into the late beats.* They went to that much effort! No wonder those records are so good.

#85—THINK OF DYNAMICS AS ADDING AND SUBTRACTING ENERGY

WHY IT MAKES YOU MORE USEFUL:

This greatly expands the list of things you can do to add dynamics.

WHAT TO DO:

Think of dynamics NOT as just loud and soft, but as *adding and subtracting energy.* This is a big switch in thinking, most likely, but it's an important and valuable one. A big chorus needs more *energy*, not just more volume. A soft verse needs less *energy*, not just less volume. Thinking this way expands your toolbox:

Long tones drain energy/Short tones add energy
Fewer notes drain energy/More notes add energy

Playing softer drains energy/Playing louder adds energy

Coming into a big chorus, start clipping the notes short as you strum the guitar, or strum faster. Coming out of the chorus, into the verse, hit one long chord and let it ring through the last two measures of the chorus.

THOUGHTS:

If you're leading a band, or everyone is looking to you for cues, you can telegraph a LOT of useful information just by the way you play. Even musicians with wandering minds, buried in their instrument, head down—even these musicians will hear that the energy is draining out of a section.

When everyone onstage does this, the effect is powerful.

Tip for keyboard players: If you play the organ, even the organ sound on a keyboard, use the Leslie Speaker Effect to add and subtract energy. The Leslie Speaker has rotating baffles and horns that speed up and slow down. The effect on your keyboard mimics this, usually by rolling a mod wheel up and down on the left side of the keyboard. Roll it up and you'll hear the rotating effect speed up (which adds energy), roll it down and it slows again (subtracting energy).

#86—PLAY LONGER NOTES TO SUBTRACT ENERGY

WHY IT MAKES YOU MORE USEFUL:

You can help bring the energy of a song down, when needed (Remember: energy is another word for 'dynamics')

WHAT TO DO:

This is an expansion of the entry about dynamics, but it's an important thought.

When the energy in a song needs to diminish, hit a note or a chord and hold it. While you're holding the note, nothing is happening and the song loses energy. Use this, for instance, coming out of a big chorus. As the chorus is ending and you're headed into a verse that's quieter, play long notes or chords and hold them.

THOUGHTS:

You can really take advantage of this if you're leading a band. Play long notes, hold long chords, and everyone will *feel* this. They'll feel it and respond (we hope). Lastly, even if everyone else is ignoring what's going on, pounding on through the whole song at the same energy level, at least YOU aren't, and it might help.

I do this when I'm leading the worship band at my little church. The drummers who play with me are good listeners (sometimes...), and we don't get much time to rehearse. So if I want to bring the feel of the song down, I'll just hit a chord and hold it. They hear this right away, and start pulling back. It works so good that I don't write dynamic markings in the music, not even 'PLAY THIS VERSE SOFTLY', as I've done in the past. I just cue them with what I'm playing.

#87—SHORTEN NOTES TO ADD ENERGY

WHY IT MAKES YOU MORE USEFUL:

You have a quick way to add and subtract energy from your playing.

WHAT TO DO:

This is really pretty simple—play shorter notes and you immediately add energy. This is useful when a tempo needs to be pulled back, but the song still needs energy. As the saying goes, 'put a little stank on it'.

There are any number of reasons a song will need more energy: You started too slow but it's too late to change, the audience is getting bored, whatever.

Speeding a song up is what immediately comes to most people's minds when they feel a song lacking energy, but it's not always a good idea. It's a *cheap* way to add energy. If the song is too slow, sure—speed it up. But that's trickier than it sounds.

It's HARD to speed up or slow down once you're locked in. But you, as an individual can have a great effect just by clipping your notes short.

Also, watch your singer, or leader. If they're signaling to go faster, they might just be feeling a lack of energy. Try shorter notes before you speed up.

THOUGHTS:

Shortening your notes, making them more staccato, is also a good way to signal the band that they need to, for lack of a better term, 'pick it up a little'. Playing in a lackluster way is an easy slough to fall into. When you hear this happening, or feel it in yourself, start with the short notes, even if only for half a verse, and see if everyone hears.

#88—TELL THE TRUTH

WHY IT MAKES YOU
MORE USEFUL:

You'll connect with people if you do them the favor of thinking they're at least as smart as you.

WHAT TO DO:

Don't try to fool them. Hide your lack of preparedness behind a clever intro, put on a funny hat to hide your mediocre voice, tell a funny story to introduce a song you don't play well —do these things and the audience will *know*, and they'll start losing respect. They lose respect, they start losing interest. This is bad. Respect them, and they will respect you.

THOUGHTS:

When I worked for The Big Church, we had everything on Sunday morning planned and timed down to the second. Literally. Everyone had a 'tech sheet' that listed all events—when each event started, who was involved, how long the segment took, etc. This approach had it's uses, but to quote Laura Ingalls Wilder:

"The trouble with organizing a thing is that pretty soon folks get to paying more attention to the organization than to what they're organized for."

One Sunday morning we finished the congregational song set and the singers grabbed their mic stands and walked off, as planned. Except...nothing happened next. I was not looking at the Tech Sheet. The Tech Sheet was sitting on the piano where I could not easily see it. We were experiencing 'dead air'. Most of the time I just *knew* what was coming next, because of the nature of the thing. Besides, we'd done the identical service twice already that morning.

Something, though, was definitely wrong—we were sitting onstage looking at the audience and the audience was sitting in the stackable chairs, looking at us. Nothing happened, nobody moved. I wanted to reach for the Tech Sheet, but I knew that ANY movement onstage would draw the attention of all 700 people in the room. Maybe ten seconds went by (a long, long time onstage) and then it hit me: the offering was next, but nobody had announced it. The lead singer was supposed to announce the offering, but she'd forgotten.

The backstage manager, Wade, leaned out from behind the curtain. The piano bench was right up against the stage right curtain leg. If I'd leaned backwards, I'd be out of sight.

Wade leaned out and I knew every eye in the place was on us.

He said, "Hey Ed."

I said, "Let me guess—they forgot to announce the offering." Wade and I were both trying not to laugh.

He said, "Right. And the director..."

I finished his sentence: "...would like me to announce the offering."

Wade slapped me on the shoulder and said, "Right again. You're on, buddy."

I didn't have a mic, so I pushed back the bench and walked out to the lip of the stage. I was grinning. The audience saw my grin and started laughing. Everybody *knew* we'd messed up. By the time I made it the 15 feet out to the edge, the audience was laughing, applauding, whistling, etc.

I made a motion for them to calm down with one hand, and motioned them to keep applauding with the other. When they finally calmed down, I shouted, "We forgot to announce the offering. So ushers, now is the time." They looked uncertain. I said, "Right now, guys. Stand up right now—this is the only signal you're going to get." They looked uncertain. I said, "That's it, right now—stand up, start passing the plate." To the congregation I said, "We're going to play a song for you while they pass the plates, but I have to get back to the piano first. So talk amongst yourselves and we'll be back up and running in a minute here." More laughter and applause.

Everyone relaxed, because (in that instance, at least), I told the truth. Be yourself. Be human. Prepare, work hard, and then don't take yourself so darned seriously.

#89—LEARN TO RECOVER

WHY IT MAKES YOU MORE USEFUL:

It keeps you in the song when things go wrong.

WHAT TO DO:

Keep your cool. You're probably not in all THAT much trouble. If you make a mistake, just plow right through it. Remember, the audience does NOT KNOW what you planned to play, and very likely will not hear things going pear-shaped. If you get lost, your hands will very likely pull you along for at least a short while. While this is happening, THINK. Think, listen and find your place. Smile. If someone else has messed up, turn to them and *play them out of it.* By that, I mean you should play a little more rhythmically, a little more deliberately. Maybe even sing their part to them. The worst thing you can do is panic. Panic leads to train wrecks. At the very, very worst, you'll have to stop the song and start up again. Nobody wants that to happen, but the audience will understand, for the most part. They all make mistakes on THEIR jobs, and it might just endear you to them.

THOUGHTS:

The audience takes its cues from you. If *you're* nervous, *they're* nervous. If you're calm, they're calm. Make a mistake? Laugh about it. You laugh, they laugh.

#90—FLIP THE SWITCH

WHY IT MAKES YOU
MORE USEFUL:

It makes you consistently the best you can be.

WHAT TO DO:

Flip the 'ON' switch and give it your all. Tell yourself, *every time you play,* that *this* time, *this* performance, *this* will be the best one you ever did. No holding back, no coasting, no excuses. You have to practice doing this, but you can get yourself to the point that it becomes habit. No sleeping through anything—*EVER.*

THOUGHTS:

I learned this lesson kinda hard, but I owe a debt to the guy who taught it to me. I was in the recording studio, making a record with a band back in the early 80's. We were laying down tracks the old fashioned way—all of us playing at the same time, looking for a take that had the magic dust on it.

The guy producing us was experienced, had worked as a kid at Chess records, running cables and plugging in mics when the Rolling Stones came through and recorded a couple of tracks. His name was Brandon Wade, and he'd been the voice on one of those 'Letter From Vietnam' records that actually made it onto the charts. I looked up to him, and had bent his ear about wanting to be a successful musician.

On one particular song I was struggling. Just kept messing up, wasn't happy with what I was playing. At the end of the 5th or 6th take, I said, "I don't know what's wrong, here...must be the barometric pressure, or something...". I thought it was a clever thing to say.

Thirty seconds later Brandon came charging out of the booth, angry and headed in my direction. With his finger in my face, he shouted at me:

"I thought you wanted to be a professional. I thought you wanted to be a CRAFTSMAN. That's what you told me. If that's what you want, you'd better STOP making excuses and start learning to give it your best EVERY SINGLE TIME. Whatever you have to do, wherever you have to go in your head, you'd better learn to reach down deep and FLIP THE SWITCH when that red recording light comes on. EVERY SINGLE TIME. If you can't do that, if you can't make it happen when it needs to happen, then somebody who CAN do that will come and TAKE YOUR PLACE. Let's do it again, and this time, MAKE IT HAPPEN."

I was speechless as he stormed back into the booth. The other guys where saying, "Hey, Ed, we're really sorry. He shouldn't have talked to you like that. He was out of line."

But I was so scared, embarrassed and angry that I was really, *really* pumped up. And guess what: I played a great take the next time around.

And then I went home and thought about it. Was he right? Up to that point I'd always thought...I dunno...that I had to be *inspired* to play really good. Could it be that I could play my best every time by just...pumping myself up? So I started trying it. Every time I played I'd raise my breathing rate, psych myself up and charge into whatever I was playing. Even the slow, soft songs—I played them with as much passion, accuracy, humanity and feeling as I could muster. After a while, it started to become habit, and I was on my way to, if not playing like one, at least *acting* like a professional.

#91—DO THE JOB
ONLY YOU CAN DO

WHY IT MAKES YOU
MORE USEFUL:

It capitalizes on your strengths and sets you apart.

WHAT TO DO:

The same thing that separates one 'artist' from another is the same thing that will separate you from those around you trying to do the same thing—your unique qualities. You will certainly, as time goes on, discover that you're a little (or a lot) better than most people at some little (or big) thing. When you figure out what that is, use it. This doesn't have to be anything huge—just some thing you do particularly well.

THOUGHTS:

I ran a cover band for 6 or 7 years, and I learned the peculiar things about the people who played with me. Here's what I did to help them shine, to do the things only they could do:

Bob, on drums, could sing and play at the same time and make it look easy. He had a good voice for lead, and it was a little bit of a novelty to watch him play and sing. A crowd pleaser. On one song, Three Dog Night's 'Mama Told Me Not To Come', he did a dead-on impression of the singer on the record. We actually had someone ask us if he was the guy who used to sing with Three Dog Night.

Roland, on guitar, was a very, very good lead player, with all kinds of great licks and soloing material. He loved blues and old jazz. The audience loved to watch him.

Tim, on bass, was very lively onstage, and could cover just about any style, including slap-bass.

Molly, on vocals, had a *killer* voice, full of character and power. And she was just sooooo cool onstage. I could see the men working up their nerve to talk with her during breaks, and the women ALL wanted to be her friend.

I doubled on both keys and guitar, doing a good job on both—something you don't see all the time.

So every song we considered doing, I looked for ways I could use those particular talents to the best effect. Bob and Molly would trade off singing, I'd wear my guitar around my neck while I played keys, moving between them, Roland got a long solo, Tim would open a song with a blistering slap-bass line. Even if we had to twist a song a little to accommodate all this, it was worth it. What we ended up with was a very, very strong sound, and one that was fairly recognizable.

Not every band leader will do this for you, so think about what you might be able to do for the ensemble you find yourself in. Don't be afraid to let that peculiar light of yours shine.

#92—CHANGE
YOUR DEFINITION
OF SUCCESS

*WHY IT MAKES YOU
MORE USEFUL:*

You leave the pressure of perfectionism behind and focus on a real world goal, one that's pretty easy to measure.

WHAT TO DO:

Aim at pleasing the people that it's important to please. (Hint: it's not you.)

When the audience is moved, when the people you play with onstage like what's happening, then you've succeeded. Period. These things truly represent success, because *this is what gets you asked to play again. This is what makes you useful. This is how you're actually graded in your effort.*

Playing really fast, playing really loud, playing obscure songs nobody's ever heard of, playing only songs you like, being the coolest person onstage, playing your part with no mistakes —all these things revolve around making YOU happy at the expense of everybody else. NOBODY likes players and singers like that. Nobody.

THOUGHTS:

I learned this late in life, and I wished I'd seen it earlier. Playing only to please yourself is a lonely road, full of frustration. I did a fair amount of it, even early on with my cover band (which I started in my 50's). I wanted to do the songs I really liked, but to my frustration, the audience didn't care what I liked. They cared what THEY liked. (Imagine that...) They dressed up, they left the house, they paid for food and drinks, and then expected something that pleased *them*. Such a simple thing, and so hard for me to embrace.

One night we played a medley I'd been DYING to play —Paul Revere & The Raiders 'Kicks' paired up with their song 'Hungry'. Oh man, it was so much fun in rehearsal. But onstage...crickets—people using the bathroom, going outside for a smoke, not dancing. I was so disappointed. We tried it once or twice more, but the medley was a clunker. We played it GREAT —no doubt about that, but nobody cared. If our goal was to play something only *we* liked, we succeeded. But if we were there to please an audience, well, we failed with those two songs. I reluctantly cut them from the set lists.

Listen—if the audience likes it, *you've succeeded.* Period. That's it—that's the definition of success. Yeah, you can beat yourself up a little because you missed things during a couple of songs, but honestly, I've watched as we butchered songs onstage and had people shoving each other out of the way to dance.

Too many musicians walk off the stage thinking, "I didn't play well. I need to practice more." Instead, they should be asking themselves if the audience liked what they played or didn't like what they played. If the audience loved it, figure out why and figure out how to do more of that.

#93—THINK LIKE
YOUR LISTENER

WHY IT MAKES YOU
MORE USEFUL:

You'll be more in tune with the audience, and when you're more in tune with the audience you'll understand better what to play and how to play it.

WHAT TO DO:

Try to listen with *their* ears. Imagine yourself walking in the door, sitting down, ordering something to drink, talking with your friends, waiting for the music to start. What do you hope for? What would be fun or entertaining or uplifting to hear? How loud should the music be?

If you're playing for dancers, they want to hear a song they know, and they want it to *feel good*. They don't want long solos, self indulgent introductions, or your weird twist on the song.

If they're dining, they don't want you trying constantly

to draw their attention, and they don't want it so loud they can't talk with their friends.

If they're sitting in a pew, they want to be drawn in by the music, to be led someplace.

In short, they're not there to watch you entertain yourself.

THOUGHTS:

I came to the club/bar/dance scene very late in life. We played a killer version of Dick Dale's 'Misirlou', and one night, after playing several good dance tunes in a row, we stopped and I started to introduce the song. I was fascinated by the story of Dick Dale, renting a ballroom in Southern California and playing his music the first week for a handful of kids, and a month later playing for *thousands* of kids. I wanted everyone to get the historical perspective. I had whittled it down to maybe four sentences, but I never even finished the first sentence. I no more than started when a woman on the dance floor rolled her eyes, threw her hands up in the air and said, "OH COME ON. JUST *PLAY.*" I'd interrupted her fun to give what sounded like a lecture to her. I learned that night that the ONLY thing those dancers wanted was dance music.

#94—LISTEN FOR
THE MAGIC

WHY IT MAKES YOU
MORE USEFUL:

When you can do this, you're moving beyond mechanics, into art.

WHAT TO DO:

Keep an ear open for what moves you. Don't overthink it, just ask yourself if what you're playing, or hearing, has that... that magic. That thing that moves you and other people. Maybe it's the feel of a song, maybe it's just one little passage in a song, maybe it's a cool lick on your instrument. Keep this thought simmering on a back burner all the time—in rehearsal, onstage, when you're thinking how a song should be presented. When you're listening to music, be aware (this takes practice) of being moved. If you can identify the building blocks of that cool thing, you're onto something very, very valuable.

Most of the time you're a craftsman, not an artist. But every once in a while you'll find a little magic, *but only if you're listening for it.*

THOUGHTS:

A guitarist named John McLaughlin, pretty famous in his day, said that when he was out on tour, playing live concerts, there would be these little moments, maybe 30 seconds long, where he and the others onstage with him would totally transcend what they normally played and it would just be pure magic. He said he couldn't explain it, and no matter how hard they tried, they couldn't get it back by trying harder. It just happened.

Frank Zappa, the weird, eclectic and *enormously* talented musician said that he would record everything his band played on tour, and when they got home he would listen to all those hours of his guitar solos. He'd find maybe 15 seconds here and there that had something really interesting going on, and he would look into these to see if they could be developed.

What I'm saying here is that for the most part, you can't make magic happen. But you can learn to listen for when it's happening, and see if there's something there you can capitalize on. At the very least, you can enjoy it while it's happening.

#95—TAKE RESPONSIBILITY FOR WHAT YOU PLAY

WHY IT MAKES YOU MORE USEFUL:

It makes you an adult, and you'll improve.

WHAT TO DO:

Always ask yourself if what you're playing is *working.* Always. Think, listen—does it fit in, move the song down the road, *get the job done*? If not, change it. Don't ask, just do it. Whatever you do, don't mindlessly regurgitate what was on the recording. You might, after thinking and listening, decide that the part on the recording is useful, but *don't assume it.*

THOUGHTS:

I was about 13 yrs old and sitting on the organ bench at my teacher's house in Borculo, MI. In front of me was a piece of music I'd practiced all week. I was pretty sure I knew it, but was unsure of the tempo. The tempo marking wasn't a metronome number, it was just a word. Allegro or Andante, or something.

I said, "How fast should this go?"

She said, "You're the one playing it. You decide."

Whoa, no, I thought. That's not how this works. It's either the right tempo or it's not. I decide? Everything about this song was decided about five million years ago when it was written. My job is to play it *correctly.* What if I decide wrong?

She was actually a little stern with me, unusual for her. She insisted I play it at the tempo I thought best. I did, and she approved. *She approved.*

Looking back, this was a big, big moment for me. I can still feel the, I dunno...*freedom,* 50 years later. She gave me permission to take it (and by extension, everything else I played) where *I wanted to take it.* She validated *my* input into it. By playing it my own way, however, I also opened myself up to criticism. Playing it *their way* meant I only had to obey orders, correctly execute the assigned duties. Playing it *my* way meant somebody had the right to say they thought it was wrong. Scary, grownup stuff. Mrs. Evans helped me take a step toward real musicianship.

The good news: you can play a song any way you want.
The bad news: you can play a song any way you want.

The Music Police are not in the room. You're on your own, and you should shoulder that responsibility. Your attitude should be, "I, we, are going to make this song *work*." If you're in a situation where somebody else is making decisions, work on the 'easier to get forgiveness than permission' plan.

And listen—when you make a decision and change something, *own it.* If it doesn't work, change it back and admit your mistake. Always go home thinking, 'Well, I did my best'.

#96—FLOAT ABOVE
THE MUSIC

WHY IT MAKES YOU
MORE USEFUL:

When you have a good overview of what's going on, you find your place in it all more easily.

WHAT TO DO:

I couldn't think of another way to put this, but I think the word 'float' works pretty good here. Make a conscious effort, as you play, to stand back and ask 'what's going on here?'. Observe everything—the audience, the room, the sound, the feeling of the band. Is everything going in the basic direction it should be? If not, what's wrong?

(Keep in mind—if you're onstage or at rehearsal and still fiddling with equipment, trying to figure out the chords, etc., you'll never get to the 'floating above' stage.)

THOUGHTS:

One thing drives another and everything is connected, so when you're in this mode you're ready to hear, see, feel and respond. When the sound is wrong—too loud, too soft, harsh, mixed poorly—it affects the audience. If the audience's attention is wandering, why is that? Make it a practice to keep a running check on all this, sort of at a back-of-the-brain level. Look for a band member that's struggling with a bad attitude. Look for an audience member that is (or might be) disruptive.

One night at the club, it was midnight and we were starting our last set. A little less than an hour to go, and I was tired. The crowd had thinned out, and I was looking forward to maybe not having to spend so much energy on the last hour.

Two minutes into the first song of that set I heard a thumping sound. Was in the PA system? But then it seemed to be coming from...outside? I looked over my shoulder, out the window, and saw a party bus disgorging 15 or 20 young women. It was a bachelorette party.

I knew they would flood the dance floor, already be drunk and wanting to dance. Immediately, while I was playing I began rearranging the last set in my head. I decided which songs would not fly, which high-energy numbers we could pull in from earlier in the evening (we didn't have an endless supply of those), etc. Also, I gave myself a pep talk—I needed to rev up the energy, personally. Yeah, it was unexpected, and maybe a tiny bit disappointing, but that was the gig. The restaurant had hired us *for just that job—to keep the dancers dancing.* So yeah— we got asked back. We were useful. That happened, in part, because I kept my eyes on the big picture and was ready when the ladies stumbled in the door.

#97—LEARN TO COUNT

WHY IT MAKES YOU MORE USEFUL:

It's half the battle. You know, the rhythm half of 'rhythm and harmony'.

WHAT TO DO:

Work on your counting, on your sense of rhythm, until it's second nature. You should be able to tap your foot on the beat no matter what you're doing with your hands. It's really not that complicated—it's whole notes, half notes, quarters, eighths, etc., and their corresponding rests in varying combinations. Get a book that gives you basic rhythms to practice, and start slow, using a metronome. Practice tapping the rhythms on your knee, or the table, with your foot keeping time. Count out loud. Spend maybe 15 minutes a day doing this and you will improve GREATLY.

If you want to move on from there, take a scale—the blues scale, for instance—and play one note for every rhythmic hit in the exercise.

THOUGHTS:

When you can do this you will have made great strides toward telegraphing the feel of the song. Tricky passages will no longer be quite so tricky and you'll learn a song much faster.

#98—LEARN TO HEAR
IN MULTIPLES OF TWO

WHY IT MAKES YOU
MORE USEFUL:

You will find (and keep) your place more easily.

WHAT TO DO:

This is the default mode for everyone. We naturally hear things in sets of two, four, eight and sixteen. Maybe a better way to say this would be to say that you *feel* sets of 2, 4, 8, and 16. Test yourself by listening to songs and counting out bars. You'll nearly always hear those multiples of two. In fact, count out the bars in a song, then listen again and see if you can just *feel* the end of the phrase coming. Even when there's an extra bar someplace, you will then hear it as the exception, and therefore more easily accommodate it.

THOUGHTS:

When you can hear and feel those sets going by, you can put yourself on autopilot during a song. Is somebody taking a solo? If you make those passages 8 or 16 bars, you can disengage a little and put your mind to work on what you're playing. Or waving at your mom, whatever.

#99—DEVELOP A THICK SKIN

WHY IT MAKES YOU MORE USEFUL:

It will keep you from developing a bad attitude, which turns you into someone nobody wants to be around.

WHAT TO DO:

Take the long view. Yes, you will spend some time on-stage with idiots. Yes, you will occasionally be misunderstood or treated poorly. Decide *ahead of time* that you're not going to let this stuff get under your skin.

THOUGHTS:

I wish I'd done better at this over the course of my performing life. I've had a few bad moments, letting things get to me. But overall, the more easy-going my attitude, the better things have been.

So, you know, if you want to sit at the grown-ups table, learn to take a hit.

#100—GET BETTER AT PLAYING WHEN YOU CAN'T HEAR YOURSELF

WHY IT MAKES YOU MORE USEFUL:

You won't be that needy musician who hogs up the sound check with whiny demands. Also, the sound guys will *love* you. When the sound guys love you, they're more inclined to act on your requests.

WHAT TO DO:

This is really about being able to pick your part out of a messy, busy mix. As I've said elsewhere, keep it simple. This will help greatly. Also, work on your ear training so you're more confident that you're playing good notes. Work on this at home by setting your instrument really low and playing along to a loud track. If you practice this, you can get much, much better at picking your sound out of the noise.

THOUGHTS:

At a concert early on in my life of playing onstage, I had to play an entire concert without hearing myself at all. Yeah, I was a little miffed, but I decided to take it as a challenge. At the end of the night, I was a little surprised—it went pretty good. Now, these were songs our band had rehearsed over and over, so that helped a lot. Still, I went away with a little more confidence.

#101—STOP THINKING OF EVERYTHING MUSICAL AS COMPLETELY MYSTERIOUS

WHY IT MAKES YOU MORE USEFUL:

It makes you a craftsman instead of waiting around for the music gods to inspire you.

WHAT TO DO:

Learn how music works. Don't be content to let it be a mystery. That's just lazy. There IS mystery in music, but YOU are nowhere NEAR that point. Knowing how the music goes together, seeing the whole picture, understanding all the parts, speaking the language—THIS is where you live. THIS is what makes you a great ensemble player. Playing whatever you feel like playing right in the moment makes you, well, pretty useless.

THOUGHTS:

It's a rookie move to say, "I don't like to know what I'm doing. I just like to feel the music and play whatever comes out my hands." I've known musicians like that all my life, and they can only do one thing—play it their own way. They can't go along. In fact, I know a *lot* of musicians who are like this.

"I don't know anything about theory and all that. It just confuses me. I just play what comes out."

As you might guess, I can see that all over their playing. They can only play solos over chords that stay in the key, only play chords in the 'regular' positions, only play something one way—the way the feeeeel it. They limit themselves because they like it all spooky and stuff.

Look, there IS mystery here, but it works at a deeper level. Coming up with something that moves people, something that pulls on people's souls—there's definitely some mystery there. That's a deeper element of artistry, but don't miss this:

Knowing what you're doing doesn't stop you from engaging the mystery of music.

You just have to make sure you're not confusing the two.

There are some famous musicians who fall into the know-nothing category , but are so supremely talented that they can afford to force everyone around them to do it their way. If that's you, what are you doing with this book in your hands?